MERRILL'S MARAUDERS

EDWARD YOUNG

ILLUSTRATED BY ADAM HOOK

Series editors Marcus Cowper and Nikolai Bogdanovic

First published in Great Britain in 2009 by Osprey Publishing
Midland House, West Way, Botley, Oxford, OX2 0PH, UK
443 Park Avenue South, New York, NY 10016, USA
E-mail: info@ospreypublishing.com

A CIP catalog record for this book is available from the British Library

ISBN-13: 978 1 84603 403 9

e-book ISBN: 978 1 84908 113 9

Editorial by Ilios Publishing Ltd, Oxford, UK (www.iliospublishing.com)
Cartography: Bounford.com
Page layout by: Mark Holt
Index by Sandra Shotter
Typeset in Sabon and Myriad Pro
Originated by PPS Grasmere Ltd
Printed in China through Worldprint Ltd

09 10 11 12 13   10 9 8 7 6 5 4 3 2 1

AUTHOR'S ACKNOWLEDGMENTS

I would like to thank Mr. Robert E. Passanisi, Merrill's Marauders Association
Historian and a member of White Combat Team, 1st Battalion, 5307th
Composite Unit (Provisional), for his extensive assistance with this volume,
and for kindly giving permission to use photographs from the Association's
extensive collection. These photographs can be seen at the Association's
excellent website, www. marauder.org. I would also like to thank my sister,
Katherine Young, who acted as my interpreter on a visit to Myitkyina, and
her son, Miles Vining, for his assistance with several of the color artworks.
All photographs are from the Merrill's Marauders Association and the
National Archives. I would like to acknowledge my uncle, then 2nd
Lieutenant Charles W. Young, First Provisional Tank Group, Chinese-
American, who sparked my interest in the American Army's experience
in Burma during World War II.

ARTIST'S NOTE

Readers may care to note that the original paintings from which the
color plates in this book were prepared are available for private sale.
The Publishers retain all reproduction copyright whatsoever.
All enquiries should be addressed to:

Scorpio Gallery,
PO Box 475,
Hailsham,
East Sussex BN27 2SL,
UK

The Publishers regret that they can enter into no correspondence upon
this matter.

THE WOODLAND TRUST

Osprey Publishing are supporting the Woodland Trust, the UK's leading
woodland conservation charity, by funding the dedication of trees.

FOR A CATALOGUE OF ALL BOOKS PUBLISHED BY OSPREY
MILITARY AND AVIATION PLEASE CONTACT:

Osprey Direct, c/o Random House Distribution Center,
400 Hahn Road, Westminster, MD 21157
Email: uscustomerservice@ospreypublishing.com

Osprey Direct, The Book Service Ltd, Distribution Centre,
Colchester Road, Frating Green, Colchester, Essex, CO7 7DW
E-mail: customerservice@ospreypublishing.com

www.ospreypublishing.com

CONTENTS

MERRILL'S MARAUDERS

INTRODUCTION

During World War II the British and American armies created several specialized units of light infantry. The British Chindits, the Canadian-American First Special Service Force, the American Ranger battalions, and the 5307th Composite Unit (Provisional), better known as Merrill's Marauders, had several characteristics in common. They were intended for offensive operations, often behind enemy lines, where their speed, mobility, and use of maneuver and surprise over difficult terrain enabled them to inflict severe casualties on the enemy force. Restricted to the weapons and equipment that could be carried on a man's back or on a mule, often completely dependent on air supply, these units had to be self-reliant. Whatever challenges the terrain or the enemy put in front of them, they faced on their own. The demands placed on the men who served in these units were exceptional; they had to undergo rigorous training, demonstrate a complete mastery of their weapons and tactics, and achieve a superior level of physical fitness and mental toughness. They fought in extremes, of climate, of terrain, and in close proximity to the enemy.

A patrol from the 2nd Battalion returns to the perimeter. Lieutenant Kenneth Brattlof leads Private Anthony Callisto, followed by Private Sydney Block. (Merrill's Marauders Association)

Men of Orange Combat Team, 2nd Battalion, 5307th Composite Unit (Provisional). Volunteers all, a journalist named them "Merrill's Marauders" after their commander, Brigadier General Frank Merrill. Left to right: Thomas Dalton, Technical Sergeant Herbert Miyaski, one of the Nisei interpreters assigned to the 2nd Battalion, Frank Wonsowicz, and Sergeant Major Jack Crowley. (Merrill's Marauders Association)

The origin of Merrill's Marauders lay in President Franklin Roosevelt's commitment at the Quadrant Conference, meeting in Quebec in August 1943, to provide an American contingent to British Brigadier Orde Wingate's proposed long-range penetration force intended for offensive operations in Burma the following year. An all-volunteer force drawn from experienced infantrymen from the United States, the Caribbean, and the South Pacific, the Marauders underwent three months of intensive training in jungle fighting and Wingate's long-range penetration tactics, and then entered combat serving under Lieutenant General Joseph Stilwell in the battle to push the Japanese out of northern Burma. The Marauders were the first American infantry force to go into action on the Asian mainland. Their elite status, the nature of their operations behind Japanese lines, and their record of victories made headlines back in the United States. In three and half months of combat, the Marauders materially aided the advance of Stilwell's Chinese divisions into northern Burma. In a daring mission the Marauders captured the vital airstrip at Myitkyina, the goal of Stilwell's campaign, after a march of 100 miles over some of the worst terrain in the world. In the course of their combat in Burma the Marauders built a lasting reputation for enduring innumerable physical hardships and for their success in fighting an experienced and determined enemy. At the end, pushed beyond their physical limits, they could go no farther.

CHRONOLOGY

1943

August 19–24   Quebec Conference decision to assign an American regiment-size long-range penetration force to Southeast Asia.

September 1   General George Marshall directs the shipment of 3,000 volunteers to India, under the code name GALAHAD.

September 20   Casual Detachments 1688A and 1688B, drawn from volunteers serving in the Caribbean and the Continental United States, leave San Francisco, picking up Casual Detachment C composed of volunteers from the South Pacific and New Guinea on the way to India.

October 29–31   Casual Detachments 1688A, B, and C disembark in Bombay, India.

November 1–17   The Detachments train at Deolali Transit Camp.

November 19   The Detachments arrive at Camp Deogarh, where they undergo intensive training until January 28, 1944.

1944

January 1   The 5307th Composite Regiment (Provisional) is established.

January 3   The 5307th is released from South-East Asia Command and assigned to Lieutenant General Joseph Stilwell's Northern Combat Area Command.

January 6   Brigadier General Frank D. Merrill assumes command, with Colonel Charles N. Hunter as second-in-command. The name of the unit is changed to the 5307th Composite Unit (Provisional).

January 26–28   The 1st, 2nd, and 3rd Battalions begin moving to Ledo in Assam, completing the movement by February 9.

February 9–21   The 5307th marches 140 miles to their jumping-off point at Ningbyen in northern Burma.

February 24–March 7   First Mission: the 2nd and 3rd Battalions set up blocks along the Kamaing Road near Walawbum.

March 12–April 7   Second Mission: the 1st Battalion sets up a block near Shaduzup.

March 12–25   Second Mission: the 2nd Battalion and Khaki Combat Team, 3rd Battalion, set up a block near Inkangahtawng.

March 25–28   The 2nd and 3rd Battalions withdraw to Nhpum Ga and Hsamshingyang to prevent the advance of Japanese forces up the Tenai River valley.

March 31–April 9	The 2nd Battalion is under siege at Nhpum Ga.
April 28–May 16	Third Mission: Merrill's Marauders, with Chinese troops and Kachin irregulars, are organized into H Force, K Force, and M Force to cross the Kumon Range and seize the airstrip at Myitkyina.
May 17–19	H Force seizes the airstrip. The Chinese 150th Regiment, 50th Division, makes an unsuccessful attempt to take Myitkyina.
May 21–31	The steadily weakening Marauders fight off strong enemy counterattacks in and around the airstrip. Evacuations for wounds and disease rise to more than 100 men a day. A completely exhausted 2nd Battalion is withdrawn from Myitkyina, with most of the rest of the Marauders following thereafter.
June 1–August 3	The remainder of the 1st Battalion, 5307th, with American Combat Engineers and infantry reinforcements together with Chinese troops struggle to overcome a tenacious Japanese defense of Myitkyina, which finally falls on August 3.
August 10	The 5307th Composite Unit (Provisional) is dissolved. The remaining Marauders are reorganized into the 475th Infantry Regiment.

RECRUITMENT AND TRAINING

On September 1, 1943, General George Marshall, US Army Chief of Staff, directed that 3,000 volunteers be recruited and sent to India to form the American long-range penetration group promised to Brigadier Orde Wingate, under the code name GALAHAD. Marshall requested that 1,000 volunteers be drawn from fully trained troops, with jungle experience, from the Army Ground Forces in the Continental United States, 1,000 jungle-trained troops from the Caribbean Defense Command, and the remaining 1,000 volunteers from veterans of the fighting in the South and Southwest Pacific. The call went out asking men to volunteer for a "dangerous and hazardous" mission requiring a "high state of physical ruggedness and stamina," with no details of where the volunteers were to be sent. The War Department decided that this volunteer unit would be allocated for a mission of up to three months' duration and would not receive any replacements during that time. Based on the experiences and casualty rates of Wingate's first Chindit expedition, the War Department fully expected that by the end of its period of operations the unit could well be so completely exhausted that it would need to be withdrawn and reconstituted.

The volunteers from the Army Ground Forces came from units across the country. They were highly trained, but few had combat experience. The volunteers were ordered to Camp Stoneman, in San Francisco, where they were designated Casual Detachment 1688A, the casual detachments later forming provisional battalions. From the Caribbean Defense Command, some 900 volunteers were drawn from the 33rd Infantry Regiment in Trinidad,

The Marauders were a cross section of the US Army and America, drawn from units in the Caribbean, the United States, and the Pacific. In this photo, which includes British, Chinese, and Kachin soldiers, men from 19 different national origins are represented. (National Archives)

with additional volunteers from Puerto Rico and Panama. The Caribbean contingent was hurriedly sent to Camp Stoneman to become Casual Detachment 1688B. On September 21, 1943, the two detachments sailed from San Francisco on board the USS *Lurline*, a converted luxury liner, under the command of Lieutenant Colonel Charles N. Hunter, the senior officer in the group. On the way to India, the *Lurline* stopped at New Caledonia to pick up 670 combat veterans from the 25th, 37th, 43rd, and Americal Divisions who had fought on Guadalcanal and New Georgia, and at Brisbane to pick up an additional 282 officers and men who had fought with the 32nd and 41st Divisions in New Guinea. This third contingent became Casual Detachment 1688C. The War Department had also recruited 14 Nisei, Americans of Japanese ancestry, to accompany the unit into Burma as Japanese language interpreters, where their knowledge of Japanese and their bravery would prove invaluable. All the men who volunteered for GALAHAD were experienced soldiers who had completed basic infantry training and, with few exceptions, training in their military specialties. Many had been in the army for two years or more, some as professionals, and some through the prewar draft. Though the majority lacked combat experience, they were not beginners at their trade.

The *Lurline* arrived at Bombay at the end of October. The three detachments spent three weeks at a British transit camp at Deolali, 125 miles from Bombay, before moving to their permanent training camp at Deogarh, in the central Indian state of Madhya Pradesh, where a tent camp had been established. Here the unit came under the control of South East Asia Command (SEAC) and was assigned to now Major General Orde Wingate. Once in India the Casual Detachments became formal battalions. Detachment A became the 1st Battalion under the command of Lieutenant Colonel William Osborne, a veteran of the fighting on Bataan; Detachment B became the 2nd Battalion, under the command of Lieutenant Colonel George McGee from the 33rd Infantry Regiment; and Detachment C became the 3rd Battalion under the command of Lieutenant Colonel Charles Beach, a veteran of combat in the Solomons. As the senior officer, Lieutenant

Colonel Hunter took on responsibility for administrating the still unnamed force, while Colonel Francis Brink, from the US Army General Staff Corps, was placed in charge of all training. Major General Orde Wingate provided Colonel Brink with guidance on the training regime he wanted in preparation for the long-range penetration mission. Wingate assigned several Chindit officers to Deogarh as advisors. One of his first requirements was that each battalion be split into two smaller, self-contained formations that Wingate called "jungle columns" and that the Americans called "combat teams." Each combat team consisted of a headquarters platoon, a pioneer and demolition platoon, a heavy weapons platoon with the heavy machine guns and 81mm mortars, 1.5 to 2 rifle companies, and a medical detachment. The 1st Battalion's teams were designated Red Combat Team and White Combat Team, the 2nd Battalion's Blue Combat Team and Green Combat Team, and the 3rd Battalion's Orange Combat Team and Khaki Combat Team. In addition, each battalion was instructed to organize a 55-man Intelligence and Reconnaissance

Colonel Francis Brink, left, who had experience in jungle warfare, was in charge of training the Marauders in India, while Lieutenant Colonel Charles N. Hunter, right, took on the administration of the unit. Hunter later became second-in-command of the 5307th. (National Archives)

Platoon which would be the battalion's eyes and ears in the jungle. Colonel Brink wanted to spread the combat experience of the men in the 3rd Battalion to the other units. In a move that was unpopular at the time, but that paid benefits later on, the 3rd Battalion transferred 160 soldiers and 6 officers to the 1st and 2nd Battalions receiving the same number of men in return.

Training had begun shortly after the USS *Lurline* put to sea and continued up until the time that the 5307th left for Burma. At Deogarh the Marauders underwent an intensive two-month training regime that emphasized physical conditioning, marksmanship, and the tactics and techniques of jungle fighting. The physical conditioning was constant. Brink, Hunter, and the unit's other senior officers knew that they would likely be fighting in difficult terrain.

Deogarh, India, where the Marauders underwent intensive training in jungle warfare and Major General Orde Wingate's long-range penetration tactics. (National Archives)

Mobility and speed would be critical to the success of the mission, and possibly to the very survival of the men they commanded. The ability to march long distances and arrive at a destination with more than sufficient strength to fight required that the men be in peak physical condition. In addition to daily sessions of calisthenics, the Marauders marched everywhere. Aided by a shortage of truck transport, the men marched to all their classes and training ranges, wearing packs at every opportunity. There were route marches of increasing length, by day and by night, to build endurance.

The combat veterans in the 3rd Battalion knew at first hand the value of marksmanship in the jungle and passed this knowledge on to the other battalions. In the jungle, the dense undergrowth could limit visibility and with camouflage an enemy soldier or position could be nearly invisible at more than a few yards' range. Targets were small, and fleeting, with ranges and fields of fire limited sometimes to only 10 or 20 yards. Trails were always likely to be set up for an ambush. Survival required lightning-quick reactions and precision marksmanship. It was not enough to get off the first shot; it had to be accurate. As an experienced Marine Corps officer wrote, "it's only the hits that count." Marksmanship training began with a thorough familiarization with the soldier's assigned weapon, sighting, and practice firing on a range in the five standard positions. The Marauders were given the opportunity to fire every weapon that the unit would take into combat, so that all learned to fire the BAR, the Thompson, and the .30-cal. Browning machine gun in addition to the Garand and the M1 Carbine. The 3rd Battalion veterans knew that practice firing at stationary targets on a range was no substitute for a course of snap firing against surprise targets. To practice snap firing, a series of deep pits were dug on a firing range at varying distances out to 200 yards, with a soldier in each pit holding a cardboard silhouette target attached to a pole. At the telephone command of an instructor, the soldiers in the pits would quickly raise their targets for a few seconds, and then pull them down again. A soldier using the range for practice could either take a firing position at the start of the range, lying prone, sitting, or standing, or could walk through the range, firing at the targets as they popped up. On this type of range a soldier could practice both speed and accuracy. A small number of men sharpened their skills further hunting the native deer and gazelle in the area around Deogarh. The three battalions had brought with them a large quantity of ammunition, so that there were ample supplies for marksmanship training. With the heavier weapons, the Marauders received training in the use of the bazooka and the flamethrower. Platoon leaders and NCOs were taught how to call in and direct

 TRAINING

The Marauders underwent intensive training at Deogarh in India emphasizing physical fitness, jungle fighting, and marksmanship. The marksmanship training focused on building disciplined, accurate fire as well as rapid response to a fleeting target. To this end, the battalions built field-target firing ranges. Field-target firing used cover, concealment, and surprise targets located at different ranges to provide more challenging and more realistic marksmanship training. A field-target range consisted of a number of camouflaged pits dug in at various ranges along a field 100–150 yards in length. A soldier acting as a marker would sit in the bottom of each pit with a silhouette target on a pole, connected to the range instructor by telephone. At the instructor's call, the marker would raise his silhouette above the edge of his pit for a few seconds, and then bring it down sharply. The trainee marksman could take any firing position he wanted, or in some cases, walk through the field-target range. He would have only a few seconds to locate the target, estimate the range, and get off a shot, just as he would in combat. This type of training proved to be far more effective than simply firing at stationary targets at known distances.

Marksmanship and physical fitness were important components of the training regime at Deogarh. Here a Marauder, wearing a full pack, trains his M1 Garand on a target. (National Archives)

A small team in training. Squad and platoon tactics received heavy emphasis. Although the Marauders practiced with the flamethrower, these were not used in combat. (National Archives)

the 81mm mortars. In combat with the Japanese, this heavy emphasis on marksmanship would bring results that more than justified the time and effort expended.

The men trained in the skills they would need to survive. Knowing that in the confines of the jungle the fight would often be at the squad or platoon level, Brink and Hunter put a great deal of emphasis on training the unit's platoon and squad leaders. The training covered scouting and patrolling, squad and platoon attacks against prepared positions, setting up blocks and ambushes along a trail, map reading and navigating in the jungle by day and night. In companies, combat teams, and battalions the Marauders worked on tactical problems, practiced river crossings, and held mock battles, including live firing exercises so that the men who had not been in combat could become accustomed to the sounds of combat. The heavy weapons platoons, pioneer and demolition platoons, and the communications sections conducted their own training in their special disciplines in addition to participating in the general training program. The specially selected Intelligence and Reconnaissance platoons underwent intensive training in patrolling, ambush, and jungle navigation. In the middle of December, the three battalions participated in an exercise with British troops from Wingate's Chindits to refine their tactics and work out any gaps in training. General Wingate visited the Marauders on two occasions to review their progress. Training began early in the day and often continued into the night. At Deogarh there were no facilities for recreation or entertainment and with the pressure to complete the training program in the time allotted, no leave was granted. At Christmas a sizable number of men from the 3rd Battalion decided to use their own initiative with regard to the leave policy and went AWOL, fanning out across India. It took the Military Police some time to bring them all back.

BELIEF AND BELONGING

If you could have asked ten different Marauders why they had volunteered, you would have received ten different answers. Like most other army units of that era, the Marauders were a cross section of America. They came from nearly every region of the country, from the small towns and the big cities, from lives of privilege and lives of poverty. They had been farmers, factory workers, lawyers, carpenters, teachers, clerks, and a host of other jobs and professions. The majority entered the army as draftees or members of the National Guard; only a few had been professional soldiers. Their ranks included an ex-Marine who had won the Navy Cross fighting in Nicaragua in the 1920s and a naturalized citizen from Germany who had fought with the Republican Army in the Spanish Civil War. When their country went to war, these men responded to the call. They knew why they were fighting. They were, in the main, self-confident and independent-minded, looking for something beyond the everyday. In his book *The Marauders*, Charlton Ogburn, who commanded the Communications Platoon in the 1st Battalion, wrote of his companions-in-arms "each of them had something egging him on."

When the common wisdom imparted to new soldiers is "never volunteer," it takes a certain type of individual to agree to go on a "dangerous and hazardous mission" of his own free will. Many Marauders volunteered out of simple patriotism; their country was at war, and if by volunteering they could help defeat the enemy and shorten the war then it was their obligation to do so. Other men volunteered because they were searching for adventure, a chance to put their training to the test, or simply to escape the tedium of garrison duty in the United States or the Caribbean. For some of the combat veterans of the Pacific Theater there was a feeling of obligation, that they had a responsibility to share the experience they had gained in the bitter fighting on Guadalcanal, New Georgia, and New Guinea. For others it was a matter of what the future had in store for them; they would inevitably see more combat, one way or another, so why not volunteer? Lieutenant Victor Weingartner, whose unit had experienced heavy losses on New Georgia, thought to himself, "nothing could be worse than that," and decided to volunteer.

A sense of belonging took time to develop. Brought together from a host of different units, hurriedly shipped to India, and thrust into an intensive training program, there was little opportunity for the men to coalesce as a unit beyond their own company or battalion, and few aids to the process. For months the unit had no designation at all, no formally appointed commander, and none of the paraphernalia that go into building a sense of identity, such as a patch or emblem. During the months in training there was only one regimental formation. The men considered themselves as belonging to Casual Detachment A, or B, or C, or later as a member of A (1st), B (2nd), or C (3rd) Battalion; few even knew that the project had the code name GALAHAD. When the unit did receive a proper designation, it was not inspiring to say the least and was almost universally hated. Toward the end of December Lieutenant Colonel Hunter pushed a formal designation of the unit through the China-Burma-India Theater bureaucracy. On January 1, 1944, the 5307th Composite Regiment (Provisional) came into being, using a block number the CBI Headquarters had allocated. Five days later, when Brigadier General Frank Merrill took command, the designation was changed to the 5307th Composite Unit (Provisional), because a brigadier general could

Lieutenant General Joseph Stilwell, left, relaxes with Brigadier Frank Merrill, commander of the 5307th. Stilwell faced enormous challenges in his campaign to push the Japanese out of northern Burma. His perceived indifference to the Marauders created bitter resentment. (National Archives)

not command a regiment. To some of the volunteers, "Five-Three-Oh-Seventh" sounded like a postal address, or worse, a quartermaster unit, not an infantry regiment. The name that became forever associated with the 5307th, "Merrill's Marauders," bestowed on the unit by James Shapley, a correspondent for *Time* magazine, was unknown to many of the men of the unit until after they had been withdrawn from combat. Pride came after the fact.

What bound the Marauders together was shared adversity. Charlton Ogburn wrote that his time with the Marauders was "the worst experience I have ever been through... There was the hunger, the exhaustion, the drenchings, the disease, the sores, the denial of every comfort and amenity." The danger was constant. For most of their time on campaign, the Marauders were operating behind Japanese lines, with no friendly troops on their flanks. There was no knowing when the column might be attacked, or what might be around the next bend in the trail. Apprehension added to the mental strain of physical discomfort, as did the sense of isolation. For months the Marauders had little news of the outside world, or even the progress of their own campaign. The soldiers were rarely informed about what was going on. Technical Sergeant Robert Passanisi remembered that "all you knew was the daily hardship. You had no knowledge of results, only your little window in your own column." And once in the jungle, there was no alternative but to keep up, to stay with the column, and keep doing your job, for the Marauders had to rely on each other to survive. There was a feeling, too, that having volunteered, you had to take whatever came your way. As the campaign went on, the men gained a sense of pride in their ability to overcome the hardships they faced and in their successes in combat with the Japanese. Many Marauders kept going in the belief that they would be relieved after three months of combat. The three-month period of operations was Wingate's original specification for his long-range penetration groups and the basis for the War Department's instructions to the China-Burma-India Theater Headquarters. This idea of three months and then relief began to circulate among the Marauders during their training and became an article of faith, to be reinforced when General Merrill told his officers that the unit would be relieved once it had captured the airstrip at Myitkyina. When this did not materialize, the effect on morale was devastating.

The other strong bond among the Marauders was a shared sense of resentment toward Lieutenant General Joseph Stilwell's Northern Combat Area Command headquarters, and especially toward Stilwell himself. This feeling of bitterness grew as the campaign wore on. The Marauders gained the impression that their own army in the theater was largely indifferent to their presence, their living conditions, or their fate. While Major General

Orde Wingate and Admiral Lord Louis Mountbattan, SEAC Commander, visited the Marauders during their training in India, Stilwell never did. Stilwell stood by the roadside when the Marauders marched over the Ledo Road into Burma, but did not bother to talk with the men marching past; they did not see him again until the capture of Myitkyina airfield. Word of strained relations between the senior officers of the Marauders and the Northern Area Combat Command filtered down to the troops, adding to the perception of an indifferent higher command. Despite all the hardships the men endured, and the evident success of their missions, the Marauders received no decorations or promotions until after the capture of Myitkyina, which gave them the impression that Stilwell cared little about what they had achieved. Charlton Ogburn spoke of the "what-the-hell-did-you-expect-anyway spirit that served the 5307th in place of morale." Despite this, the Marauders continued on, griping like hell, but always doing the job they were given.

APPEARANCE

The Marauders were given a certain degree of independence in choosing the clothing and equipment for their mission. Nearly all items were standard US Army issue for tropical service. There was one constraint: a man had to carry whatever he chose to take with him. Once behind enemy lines, there would be no return to a base camp. There was a strong incentive to get rid of as much weight as possible. Some items that seemed necessary at the beginning were quickly discarded once the marching had begun.

The standard uniform for the majority of the Marauders was the darker green M1943 HBT (herringbone twill) cotton shirt and the second pattern M1943 HBT pants. The M1943 HBT shirt featured two large breast pockets, while the HBT pants featured two large cargo pockets on the thighs, useful for storing K-rations or hand grenades. Some soldiers chose to wear the 1943 version of the HBT one-piece work uniform, though the first bout of dysentery often proved this to have been a poor choice as the one-piece uniform was not easy to remove quickly. Each soldier was issued with one shirt and one pair of trousers. An olive drab vest and three pairs of cotton socks were included. These uniforms saw hard use. The Marauders were almost always on the move. There was little chance to bathe, and even less opportunity to wash clothes. Constant crossing of rivers and streams, rain, and the humidity of the jungle made it hard to keep clothing dry and not subject to mildew and rot. New uniforms were provided every three to four weeks, if possible. In the hills of

Marauders taking a break during their march up the Ledo Road to their jumping-off point in the upper Hukwang Valley. The men are wearing the M1943 herringbone twill (HBT) shirt and pants, with leather ankle boots and M1938 canvas leggings. (National Archives)

northern Burma, where the Marauders were to operate, the nights can be quite cool. To provide some extra warmth, the 5307th acquired Indian-made light wool pullovers. Lighter than a sweater, some soldiers wore these khaki-brown pullovers instead of their HBT shirts.

The HBT floppy-brimmed fatigue hat, nicknamed the "Daisy Mae," was commonly worn during training, while marching, in camp, and sometimes on patrol. Each soldier wore his "Daisy Mae" according to his own taste or inclination, with the brim up or down, the hat full on, or pushed back on the head. All soldiers had an M1 steel helmet and helmet liner. Some marched wearing their helmets, while some attached their helmets to their packs, wearing them only in combat. Some soldiers kept a knit wool cap for the cool nights in the hills. For footwear, each Marauder was issued with the standard brown leather ankle boot with the M1938 canvas leggings, which provided some protection against leeches. The Marauders were also issued with jungle boots, made of canvas with rubber soles, which were better for walking through the many streams and rivers that had to be crossed. The upper part of the jungle boot was sometimes cut off to avoid chafing the calf, making them ankle boots. The jungle boots were tied to the pack and pulled on when needed. The other standard item was a nylon poncho with a drawstring that doubled as a groundsheet.

EQUIPMENT

During training the staff drew up a standard combat load for the clothing and equipment an individual Marauder would need on the mission. Brigadier General Merrill told the soldiers that they could discard what they did not consider necessary, and that as long as they could carry their required load of ammunition, they could add other items of equipment of their own choice. The early war "Improved M1910" webbing was the foundation for the average Marauder rifleman's web gear, beginning with the M1938 cartridge belt, which had two six-pocket sections, each pocket containing one eight-round clip for the M1 Garand rifle. Officers and soldiers who did not carry a rifle wore the plain webbing M1936 pistol belt, with various attachments. The cartridge or pistol belt carried two canteens, with canvas covers and a one-pint canteen cup. Every soldier carried an M1910/1942 first aid pouch, which contained a field dressing, gauze, sulphadiazine tablets, morphine, and a suture kit. In addition, the 5307th's medical officers developed a special jungle medical kit, a small canvas pouch containing atabrine tablets to counter malaria, halazone tablets for water purification, and, when available, vitamin tablets. The men were required to keep these jungle medical kits stocked and to use them regularly. Each squad also had several snakebite kits. The M3 trench knife with a reinforced leather scabbard was issued as part of the soldier's combat load and attached to the webbing belt. The riflemen carried additional ammunition in six-pocket cloth bandoliers. Browning Automatic Rifle (BAR) men carried their ammunition in the M1937 automatic rifleman's belt, with six pockets holding two 20-round magazines each. Those armed with a Thompson submachine gun carried their magazines in a canvas pocket holding five magazines. M1936 web suspenders, which hooked onto the webbing belt, helped carry the load.

The Marauders were given considerable freedom to choose the equipment they wanted to carry on the campaign. These Marauders have various items tied to their M1928 haversacks with nylon parachute cord and stuffed in their pockets. A full load of pack, ammunition, and rations could weigh more than 45 pounds. (Merrill's Marauders Association)

To carry their other gear the Marauders were given their choice of three different kinds of packs: a pack board, the standard M1928 haversack, and the M1943 jungle pack. Despite its shortcomings, most soldiers chose the M1928 haversack. Contained in the haversack, or attached to it, was a variety of additional equipment, depending on the individual's preferences and willingness to carry the weight. Most carried the M1910 entrenching tool in its canvas carrier. Every soldier was issued a wool blanket, which was wrapped in the waterproof poncho and folded around the haversack. Almost every soldier quickly acquired a length of nylon rope cut from parachutes to tie the poncho/blanket and jungle boots to the haversack; many carried an additional 20 feet or so of nylon rope, which was useful for setting up temporary shelters in the nightly bivouac area. American-made M1942 machetes with an 18-inch blade were issued as part of the standard equipment, but the Gurkha kukri knife was much preferred, and much coveted for its comfortable fit in the hand and the greater ease in carrying its curved blade. Once behind enemy lines, the standard metal mess kit was quickly discarded; the kits made noise while moving in the jungle, and as the Marauders subsisted almost entirely on K-rations, there were few opportunities for cooked meals. A spoon, trench knife, and canteen cup were sufficient. For river crossings, the Marauders were issued with small 1 foot by 6 inch flotation bladders, which made wonderful

MARAUDER UNIFORMS AND WEAPONS, 1944

With some exceptions, the Marauders used standard American Army mid-war equipment and weapons. Individuals were given a degree of choice over what clothing and equipment they wanted to take with them into the jungle, although all were required to carry with them a standard load of individual ammunition and rations. (**1**) This Marauder rifleman is wearing the M1943 late pattern herringbone tweed (HBT) green cotton fatigue shirt and pants with thigh cargo pants. He wears the Army M-1 metal helmet, leather ankle boots, and canvas leggings. The M1938 12-pocket cartridge belt carried ammunition clips for his M1 Garand rifle, one or two canteens, and a small first aid kit. Most Marauders carried some type of knife, either an M3 trench knife (**2a**) or a personal hunting knife (**2b**) brought from the United States. While special jungle packs were available, most Marauders chose the M1928 haversack (**3**) to carry their gear. A blanket roll consisting of a light wool blanket and poncho or shelter half was tied around the top of the haversack. An M1910 entrenching tool (**4**) and 10-inch bayonet (**5**) for the M1 Garand were attached to the haversack; the former was one of the few pieces of equipment the Marauders had for digging trenches, foxholes, steps in a hillside, and cooking. This soldier has managed to acquire an Indian-made kukri knife (**6**) which he carries attached to the side of his haversack. Each Marauder was given a pair of rubber and canvas jungle boots (**7**), which many tied to their haversacks with nylon parachute cord; the rubber and canvas jungle boots were particularly useful during river crossings. The M1 Garand (**8**) was standard for riflemen. The green HBT "Daisy Mae" floppy hat (**9**) was popular. Many Marauders wore their "Daisy Mae" hats while marching or in bivouac in preference to their heavy helmets. To give some added warmth at night, which could be quite cool in the dry season and in the higher elevations, the Marauders were issued with locally made light wool jerseys (**10**), which were frequently worn in lieu of fatigue shirts. The Marauders received large numbers of the US Army M1942 machete (**11**), which was vitally necessary for cutting trails through the jungle, though most men preferred the Gurkha kukri. Since K-rations were the main ration for the Marauders, the full metal army mess kits were quickly discarded as unnecessary weight. The standard metal canteen cup (**12**) was all that was needed to heat coffee, make a stew, or a rice pudding. A spoon was the only cooking utensil needed. (**13**) K-rations constituted 80 percent of the Marauders' rations while they were on campaign. Originally intended as emergency rations only, K-rations did not contain sufficient calories to sustain the Marauders through their hard physical exertion. The monotony of K-rations made the occasional airdrops of C-rations a welcome relief. (**14**) The Mk II A1 fragmentation grenade was regularly supplied in airdrops. Each Marauder would be given five grenades at each re-supply. Two would be attached to the belt harness, and the others stuffed in pockets or in the haversack, though as the day's march dragged on and the hill climbs grew tougher, the extra grenades would often be tossed into the jungle.

9

1

5 3

6

11

2a

2b

14

12

10

U.S.

4

7

13

8

pillows when inflated. Other small items stuffed here and there were typically a compass, waterproof matches, a pocket knife, and a few personal items such as photographs or letters. Toiletries were basic; razors and toothbrushes were supplied in airdrops from time to time, but little else. When all was tied on and in place, and with rations and extra ammunition, a soldier's pack could weigh up to 60 pounds. There was little relief from this weight. A Marauder carried all his own equipment, from the beginning of the campaign to the end.

Weapons

As light infantry, the Marauders had little heavy equipment, no mechanized transport, and seldom had support from other combat arms, apart from the fighter-bombers of the US Army Air Force. They were reliant on their own organic infantry weapons, weapons that an individual soldier could carry or that could fit on the back of a mule. With two years or more of US Army service, the Marauders were already familiar with the army's standard infantry weapons. The combat veterans knew the strong and weak points of each. The training at Deogarh sharpened their skills and provided an opportunity to qualify on other weapons. Riflemen, who made up two-thirds of a battalion's strength, carried the M1 Garand semi-automatic rifle with a 10-inch bayonet fixed to the haversack. An excellent weapon, the Garand's main drawback from the Marauder's perspective was its weight. Climbing the rugged hills of northern Burma with a heavily loaded pack, grenades and ammunition, and a 10-pound rifle was no picnic. But the Garand's eight-shot clip and semi-automatic fire gave

The most common weapon among the Marauders was the heavy but powerful M1 Garand rifle. The semi-automatic Garand's eight-shot clip gave the Marauders a decided advantage over the Japanese bolt-action, five-shot Arisaka. Corporal Bernard Martin shows his M1 to a Chinese soldier along the trail to Myitkyina. (National Archives)

The Browning Automatic Rifle and the Thompson submachine gun, when combined with the M1 Garands and M1 carbines, enabled the Marauders to put out a heavy weight of fire, which proved devastating against the unsupported infantry charges the Japanese employed against them. (Merrill's Marauders Association)

the Marauders a decided advantage over the Japanese five-shot, bolt-action Arisaka rifle. Though fewer in number than the Garand, the M1 Carbine was popular for its lighter weight and its lighter ammunition. The M1 Carbine .30-cal. round's relative lack of penetrating power compared with the M1 Garand's .30-06 cartridge was less of a problem at the shorter ranges the Marauders typically encountered fighting in the jungle. With a cut-down, five-round magazine, the M1 Carbine was easier to manipulate through the jungle or along a narrow trail, and with four of the standard 15-round magazines carried as well, could contribute a good amount of firepower to a patrol.

The Browning Automatic Rifle and the Thompson submachine gun were the other main infantry weapons. The BAR was particularly favored for its rate of fire and penetrating power; it could cut through brush where the rounds from the Thompson could not. The Marauders used the M1918A2 model and a few of the shorter M1922 versions. The Thompson's lack of accuracy beyond more than 50 yards was less of an issue in the jungle. What mattered most in the type of engagements the Marauders experienced was the weight of firepower and the speed with which it could be delivered. As Lieutenant Colonel John George, who served in the 3rd Battalion, wrote in his book *Shots Fired in Anger*, "when Japanese and American patrols met head on and in mutual surprise on a jungle trail the American advantage in semi-auto weapons usually let us win heavily." The volume of fire all these individual weapons could put out, combined with disciplined marksmanship from hours of training, would prove devastating against the Japanese. The main drawback of both the BAR

The Marauders carried with them small numbers of M1903A4 Springfield sniper rifles and the M1903A3 Springfield with grenade launcher. These Marauders from the 2nd Battalion pass two dead Japanese soldiers who were killed near Walawbum after running into the battalion's Intelligence and Reconnaissance Platoon. The lead soldier carries the Springfield sniper rifle. (Merrill's Marauders Association)

The Marauders relied on the M1917A1 .30-cal. water-cooled machine guns of the heavy weapons platoons for additional firepower. This 3rd Battalion machine gun fired in support of the attempts to break through to the 2nd Battalion at Nhpum Ga. Note the thickness of the jungle behind the position, typical of what the Marauders encountered in the hills of northern Burma. (Merrill's Marauders Association)

and the Thompson was their weight. As other Army and Marine Corps BAR men did, the Marauders removed every attachment on their BARs to lighten their load.

The Marauders took with them small numbers of the M1903A4 Springfield sniper rifle and the M1903A3 Springfield with the M1 grenade launcher. The M1903A4 was barely adequate as a sniping rifle, but opportunities to use it at long distances were rare. Much of the shooting in northern Burma was done at ranges of less than 100 yards, and most often less than 50 yards, where an M1 Garand or M1 Carbine were just as good. Several Springfield rifle grenade launchers were allocated to each platoon. They were considered to be less effective in the jungle than the Japanese Type 89 grenade launcher. The Marauders also brought with them a small number of the Winchester M97 12-gauge pump-action shotguns.

For more firepower the Marauders relied on the air-cooled .30-cal. M1919A4 machine gun and the heavier .30-cal. M1917A1 water-cooled machine gun, which provided a high rate of sustained fire. Though it was

C **WEAPONS AND EQUIPMENT**

The Marauders had to carry their weapons and equipment on their backs. What a man couldn't carry went on the back of a pack animal, a horse or a mule. The Marauder riflemen carried the M1 Garand rifle; officers and specialists carried the lighter M1 carbine (**1**). The much heavier Thompson submachine gun (**2**) proved to be highly effective against Japanese infantry charges when the Marauders would open fire at 20 yards or less. (**3**) The M1918A2 Browning Automatic Rifle was the principal squad automatic weapon. Its cartridge could penetrate any vegetation in the jungle. (**4**) Each platoon was issued with a small number of Springfield M1903A3 rifles with M1 grenade launcher, though the confines of the jungle sometimes limited its usefulness. (**5**) The M1 grenade adaptor with the Mk II fragmentation grenade for the Springfield. (**6**) The Marauders were given a few of the Springfield M1903A4 sniper rifles. (**7**) The M1919A4 .30-cal. machine gun and (**8**) the M1917A1 .30-cal. water-cooled machine gun provided heavier firepower. For most of the campaign the Marauders did not have any of their own artillery. Though the 75mm pack howitzer was available, instead the Marauders relied on (**9**) the M2 60mm mortar and (**10**) the M1 81mm mortar, both effective in the jungle. (**11**) Radio communications were vital to the Marauders' survival. Each battalion carried several SCR-284 radio sets with GN-45 hand-crank generators, carried on pack animals. Without the pack mule and packhorse, the Marauders would have had to go without their heavy weapons and radios.

difficult to employ in the confines of the jungle, the heavier and more cumbersome M1917 with all its accessories could still be easily transported on the back of a mule and was an excellent defensive weapon. As Lieutenant Colonel John George noted, "mortars are an absolutely essential tool of jungle warfare." Mortars could be easily transported on pack animals and rapidly deployed in difficult terrain where pack howitzers could not be used. More importantly, mortars could be used at very close range in defense or in the attack, an absolute necessity in the jungle. The Marauders relied heavily on the 60mm M2 mortar and the more powerful 81mm M1. Only later in the campaign, when circumstances dictated, did the Marauders acquire two 75mm M1A1 pack howitzers. At Deogarh the Marauders trained with flamethrowers and the 2.36-inch M1A1 bazooka, but these were not used in combat.

Air support

Operating behind Japanese lines as they did, the Marauders were heavily dependent on air support for supply, casualty evacuation, and firepower. Everything the Marauders needed – rations, ammunition, clothing, medical supplies, grain for the pack animals – had to be supplied by air. Indeed, air supply was the lifeline that made the Marauders' tactical mobility and their entire mission possible. Orde Wingate's first Chindit expedition in 1943 had proved that a large body of troops could be supplied by air. The Marauders employed the principles and procedures the Chindits had developed. Air supply required the closest possible cooperation

Technical Sergeant Chester Degrange, Khaki Combat Team, 3rd Battalion, cleans his 60mm mortar after the battle at Nhpum Ga. Mortars were vital in the jungle, but many American soldiers thought the Japanese Type 89 grenade launcher was the more effective weapon. (National Archives)

The Marauders were restricted to weapons that could be carried on a pack animal. For most of the campaign the Marauders relied on the 81mm mortar. Here a mortar team sets up to provide perimeter defense. (Merrill's Marauders Association)

between the troops in the field, the rear echelon supply organization, and the Army Air Force troop carrier squadrons. To this end, each combat team had an air liaison officer attached to help coordinate all requests for air supply and air support. The 5307th's supply base at Dinjan, west of Ledo, prepared standard units of rations, ammunition, and other supplies based on estimated daily needs. These standard units were kept prepared and ready to move at short notice. The battalions would send in requests for a specified number of units and any other special requirements by radio. When the location and timing of an airdrop had been selected, the supplies were taken to nearby air bases and loaded onto the C-47s of the 1st and 2nd Troop Carrier Squadrons, who would be guided into the drop zones by radio operators on the ground. A regular airdrop required three to four C-47s. Colored panels would mark the drop zone, the required direction of approach, and the direction of the wind. Drop zones could be anything from rice fields, a small clearing in the jungle, or a sandbank along a river. The C-47s would make their runs at 200 feet, while the soldiers on the ground kept a sharp lookout for enemy fighters. Speed and accuracy were essential. Careful packing and special markings insured that the airdropped supplies could be rounded up and distributed in the shortest time possible. Colored parachutes identified rations, ammunition, and other supply packs. Special work details quickly removed the parachutes and airdropped packages from the drop zone. The packages would be broken open and individual units of rations and ammunition would be handed to each man as he walked by or loaded onto pack animals. In this way an entire battalion could be re-supplied in one or two hours.

The evacuation of casualties initially posed a considerable problem for the Marauders. Fortunately, the availability of L-4 and L-5 liaison planes from the 71st Liaison Squadron at Ledo provided a solution. In repeated demonstrations of remarkable flying, the liaison pilots would land in what looked like impossibly small stretches of flat ground, a rice paddy or sandbar, to pick up casualties for evacuation back to the larger military hospitals around Ledo. Air evacuation saved countless lives of badly wounded men who could not otherwise be transported back behind the lines. Knowledge that, if wounded, one had a reasonably good chance of getting back to a hospital was a big boost to morale.

There were times when, in contact with large groups of Japanese troops, the Marauders needed more firepower than their own mortars could provide. Lacking artillery, the Marauders could and did call on the A-36 Invaders and

ABOVE LEFT
The Marauders relied on regular airdrops for all their supplies of rations, ammunition, and other equipment. Packed into standard units that were readily identifiable and easily broken down, an airdrop had to be completed as quickly as possible. The C-47 pilots had to maneuver around hills and down into valleys to get to the drop zone; the kickers had to be tied to the airplane to avoid getting thrown out. (National Archives)

ABOVE RIGHT
Air evacuation was the only way the seriously wounded could be taken back to a hospital. The liaison pilots flew their L-4s and L-5s into impossibly small areas. Here an L-4 pilot checks on his stretcher patient before flying back to the rear area. (National Archives)

P-51A Mustangs from the 311th Fighter Group at Dinjan for close air support. The air liaison officers would pass on requests for air support and help coordinate and direct air strikes from the ground. Close air support was invaluable, but had its drawbacks. Fighters were rarely on call; it took time to arrange an air strike. Targets were difficult to spot in the jungle, particularly when troops were in close contact.

Communication and transport

An argument could be made that the most important pieces of equipment the Marauders took with them were the radio and the pack animal. The mission would have been impossible without them. Communication was simply vital to the control and coordination of columns moving independently through the jungle terrain, the rapid transmission of intelligence, and the coordination of air supply, air evacuation, and close air support. Radios gave the Marauder columns the ability to move independently or converge as necessary, like ships at sea. Each battalion had a long-range AN/PRC-1 radio to maintain contact with the base at Dinjin and a shorter-range SCR-84 radio to contact the C-47 transports on airdrops and the Mustangs on close air support missions. These heavy radios were transported on several mules. Every evening, after setting up camp in the bivouac area, the communications sections would unpack their radio equipment, put up their antennas on long sections of bamboo, and spend several hours sending and receiving messages, taking turns cranking the hand generators that powered the radios. At the tactical level, the battalions used the 32-pound SCR-300 (known as the Walkie-Talkie) to coordinate movement of the combat teams and the Intelligence and Reconnaissance platoons, and to request and direct mortar fire.

Pack animals were the Marauders' only means of transporting heavier equipment. Each soldier carried his own weapon, ammunition, and rations, but all crew-served weapons, the vital radios, and extra ammunition went on a mule or a horse. The 5307th was to have received 700 American mules, but the ship carrying the unit's second shipment of 340 mules was torpedoed in the

The radiomen of the 5307th marched all day then spent much of the night sending and receiving messages. Radio communication was critical to the ability of the Marauders to operate behind Japanese lines. Standing, left to right, John Egan, Lieutenant Filiak; seated, left to right, Carl Hamlic, Leon Lanphere, and Chester Dulin. (Merrill's Marauders Association)

The mules and horses that accompanied the Marauder columns carried heavy loads and suffered appallingly from wounds and exhaustion. But without them the Marauders could not have operated behind enemy lines for extended periods. (National Archives)

Arabian Sea. To replace the lost mules 340 Australian horses that had been with the Chinese troops at their training center in Ramargh arrived just before the Marauders' departure for Burma. Two pack troops were assigned to the Marauders to oversee the loading and care of the pack animals, but other soldiers, often with no experience of working with animals, had to be drafted in to help. Being a muleskinner was hard work. The mules and horses had to have their pack saddles taken off every night, then be re-saddled in the morning, pushed, prodded, and hauled up and over the steep hills and across the many streams and rivers the Marauders crossed. Few of the pack animals survived to the end of the campaign.

TABLE 1: BATTALION ORGANIZATION AND WEAPONS

	Battalion HQ	Combat Team 1	Combat Team 2	Total
Officers	3	16	16	**35**
Enlisted men	13	456	459	**928**
Total	16	472	475	**963**
Pack animals	3	68	68	**139**
Machine guns, heavy		3	4	**7**
Machine guns, light		2	4	**6**
Mortars, 60mm		4	6	**10**
Mortars, 81mm		4	3	**7**
M1 carbines	6	86	89	**181**
M1 rifles	8	306	310	**624**
Submachine guns	2	52	48	**102**
BAR		27	27	**54**
Pistols		2	2	**4**

Source: Merrill's Marauders (February–May 1944), Historical Division, War Department, 1945

ON CAMPAIGN

Mission, tactics, and terrain

At the Quadrant Conference, meeting in Quebec in August 1943, President Franklin Roosevelt, Prime Minister Winston Churchill, and the Combined Chiefs of Staff agreed on a comprehensive strategy for the re-conquest of northern Burma in 1944 in order to establish an overland supply route from Assam in northeastern India to China. The Combined Chiefs of Staff's directive to Lieutenant General Joseph Stilwell, the American commander of the China-Burma-India Theater and commander of the Northern Combat Area Command, called for the American-trained and equipped Chinese divisions under his command to advance from Ledo in Assam down the Hukwang Valley, then over the Mogaung Valley to capture the Mogaung–Myitkyina area, then advance southward toward Lashio, where a new road from Ledo, which American Army engineers were building just behind the advancing Chinese, would link up with the old Burma Road into China. The town of Myitkyina was the key, the start of the road and rail network that led south, and the site of an airfield that could shorten the air route to China over the Hump.

Stilwell's Chinese force consisted of the three regiments of the 38th Division, the 65th and 66th Regiments of the 22nd Division, and the Chinese 1st Provisional Tank Group. Facing the Chinese was the Japanese 18th Division, veterans of the capture of Singapore, under Lieutenant General Shinichi Tanaka. Tanaka had under his command the 55th, 56th, and the 114th Infantry Regiments and the 18th Mountain Artillery Regiment. Tanaka's plan was to fight a series of delaying actions against the Chinese to hold them in the Hukwang Valley until the monsoon rains came in May–June. Stilwell's Chinese forces had entered the northern end of the valley at the end of October 1943, but had made little progress against strong opposition from the Japanese 56th Regiment, who sat astride the Kamaing Road, the only road in the valley and the Japanese 18th Division's principal supply line. Tanaka found the Chinese to be lethargic, and seemingly reluctant to take advantage of opportunities to defeat the Japanese through an envelopment. Against his slower-moving opponent, Tanaka found that by using his internal lines of communications he could quickly concentrate his own forces to defeat or delay the Chinese advance, without having to worry about his own flanks. Stilwell's great

At the beginning of the campaign Lieutenant General Joseph Stilwell had two divisions of Chinese troops that the American Army had trained in India. The Chinese had a mix of American and British weapons and equipment. (National Archives)

frustration was his inability to get the Chinese units to move more aggressively. He desperately wanted American troops that would respond to his commands. He continued to press Admiral Lord Louis Mountbatten, SEAC commander, to assign the 5307th to his command.

Shifting strategic priorities and plans for the Allied offensive in Burma in 1944 led to a change in General Wingate's long-range penetration mission, which freed up the 5307th. When the 5307th became available, Stilwell asked Wingate if the unit could be assigned to his command, which Wingate agreed to. Stilwell moved quickly to bring the unit under his control. He appointed Brigadier General Frank D. Merrill, a West Point graduate who had been a language student in Japan and had spent time with the Japanese Army, as commanding officer. Merrill had been on Stilwell's walkout of Burma in 1942 and had been serving with Stilwell ever since. Merrill took charge of the 5307th on January 6, 1944; Charles Hunter was promoted to full colonel and made second in command. Stilwell ordered Merrill to complete the unit's training and get to Ledo by February 7.

In contrast to Orde Wingate's conception of the role of long-range penetration forces, Stilwell thought that these units could be better employed in short envelopments, working in close cooperation with the main force attacking the Japanese, rather than in the deep penetrations behind Japanese lines that Wingate proposed. Stilwell's plans for pushing the Japanese 18th Division out of the Hukwang Valley invariably called for an envelopment; with the Marauders, Stilwell finally had the tool he needed for the tactics he wanted to employ. Stilwell intended to use the Marauders as a blocking force, taking advantage of the Marauders' speed and tactical mobility to swing around Tanaka's flank to set up blocks across the Japanese 18th Division's supply line, squeezing Tanaka's forces between the advancing Chinese and the Marauders. Stilwell wanted to present Tanaka with the choice of staying in his position at the risk of a punishing defeat against Stilwell's numerically superior Chinese force, or fighting his way past the Marauders, and thereby giving up more territory.

With a good trail, the Marauders could march 12 or more miles in a day, but in thick jungle and in the hills where the trails barely existed, a day's march would cover a few miles at best. (Merrill's Marauders Association)

The challenge to tactical mobility was the terrain of northern Burma, an area of jungle-covered valleys and rugged hills. In the area of operations the Marauders were entering, an area of 5,000 square miles, the Kumon Range, running north–south with mountains rising as high as 10,000 feet, divided the region into two separate sections. To the west of the Kumon Range lay the broad Hukwang Valley, crisscrossed with numerous rivers and streams that flowed north into the Chindwin River. At the southern end of the Hukwang Valley, the Jambu Bum ridge separated the Hukwang from the narrower Moguang Valley, which to its south gave access to the Irrawaddy River valley. To the east of the Kumon Range lay the Irrawaddy River which flowed south from its headlands in the Himalayas, past Myitkyina, down through central Burma to the sea. A tangle of trees, underbrush, vines, and bamboo covered the valley floor. Clearings were often covered in razor-sharp Kunai grass that could grow as high as six feet. In the hills, the tropical rainforest blocked out the sunlight, though there could still be sections of dense undergrowth. The Japanese controlled the single road that ran down the Hukwang Valley, over the Jambu Bum to the town of Mogaung and on to Myitkyina. Traversing the region meant going along cart tracks and footpaths made by the Kachin people who lived in the area. In the hills, the paths were often only wide enough to walk single file. To get around the Japanese, who controlled the valleys, the Marauders had to go into the hills, and as the campaign wore on, the hills only got worse. The US Army's official history of the campaign put it this way:

> So quickly and easily described in print, these marches in north Burma were in reality exhausting struggles against every variety of obstacle. Staggering up stream beds, clawing their way between jungle growths, clinging to hillsides, their only respite a few hours on the sodden ground, their food a little K-ration gulped on the march – the infantry endured a continuous ordeal that language is really inadequate to describe.

Marching

The Marauders went directly from training into combat. At the end of January 1944 the three battalions left Deogarh, traveling by rail and boat over 1,000 miles to arrive in Ledo in Assam at the end of the first week of February. General Merrill and Colonel Hunter decided that the unit would march the 140 miles to its jumping off point at Ningbyen at the northern end of the Hukwang Valley. This 10-day march, along the newly built Ledo Road up and over the hills of the Patkai Range, served to break in men, mules, and

 DAILY LIFE

The Marauders spent most of their time marching. To get behind Japanese lines and maintain the element of surprise, the Marauders had to avoid the Japanese-controlled valleys and take to the hills, following native Kachin trails which were little more than narrow dirt tracks. Climbing up and over the hills and mountains in the Kumon Range was back-breaking work, even when there was a semblance of a Kachin trail. In some sections, the trail was too steep for the mules to climb with a full load. The muleskinners had to unpack their mules and horses, pull and prod their charges to climb up the hillside, and then go down the hillside again to bring up the loads on their own backs. Sometimes the Marauders had to hack steps out of the hillside for the mules, and set up rope guides along the trail so they could pull themselves up the trail. These climbs had to be done in the heat of the day and in the pouring rain. In the final march on Myitkyina, many mules and horses slipped off the trails and fell to their deaths below, taking with them vital equipment. At the end of each day came the knowledge that the process would begin all over again the next morning.

horses, in a foretaste of what was to be their lot for the next three and a half months. As "Stilwell's foot cavalry," the Marauders spent most of their time marching, getting to one objective, and then moving on to the next. By the end of their campaign, the Marauders had marched more than 700 miles.

The terrain dictated the distance that could be covered in the course of a day, and how difficult the day would be. With a good trail over low hills or along a valley, a column could cover 12 or more miles, but later in the campaign there were days of marching over the steep jungle-covered hills of the Kumon Range where after 10 or more hours of grueling effort a column would have covered barely a mile. The battalions traveled separately toward their objectives, sometimes splitting up into their component combat teams, with General Merrill or Colonel Hunter coordinating their movement by radio. The Intelligence and Reconnaissance Platoons went out ahead of their battalions, sometimes as much as 10 to 20 miles beyond the main column, checking the route of advance, looking for potential drop zones and bivouac areas, and always scouting for the Japanese. The battalions marched in a single file in a long column along the trail. A rifle platoon was always in the lead, followed by a full rifle company, then half of the battalion's heavy weapons platoon. The command group traveled in the middle of the column, with the medical team and the communications platoon, followed by the second rifle company and the rest of the heavy weapons platoon. Vigilance had to be constant. All along the column the men watched for any sign of the Japanese who might have slipped past the Intelligence and Reconnaissance Platoon to set up an ambush. The Marauders soon learned that the main danger lay along the trails, where the Japanese could lie in ambush; the jungle meant comparative safety. Each path leading off the main trail had to be checked for signs of ambush before the column arrived, and guarded until the last man in the column had passed by. Every bend in the trail, every site of a potential ambush, had to be approached with caution. River crossings were particularly nerve-wracking, with the men and mules wading across, vulnerable to Japanese machine-gun fire. The tension would only subside once the entire column was across and back on the trail again.

The day began before dawn. The men would rise, pack their equipment, and try to eat some breakfast. If there was time, and no Japanese were in the area, it was possible for a squad to build a small fire to heat some coffee in a canteen cup, using the waxed cardboard from their K-ration boxes. Fires were only possible at dawn and dusk, when mist and haze would mask the smoke. After breakfast, the pack animals would be loaded and the platoons would take their positions in the column, the platoons alternating in taking the point. The day's march would begin, and continue until the late afternoon, and at times well into the night. The columns would try to take a 10-minute break every hour, and at midday a short break for lunch, if they could. If there was a hold-up the column would come to a complete halt, with word passing from man to man down the length of the column to stop and pull off the trail. The mules had to be taken off the trail in pairs; the muleskinners soon learned that a mule on its own would bray loudly, but with the company of a fellow mule would remain silent. When the units at the front had cleared up the problem, word to start up again would be passed down, and then the column would move forward, like a great olive green snake making its way through the hills. At times a column would find the Japanese blocking the trail, or would need to go off the trail into the jungle to maneuver into position. Cutting a new trail through the thick undergrowth or bamboo was back-breaking work. The soldiers took turns wielding a machete or kukhri knife, making a bigger and bigger hole to pass through. This often meant making two cuts, high and low, so that the passage would be big enough for the mules and horses with their loads. And if the hills were too steep for the mules, they would have to have their packsaddles removed, and be pushed, cursed, and pulled up the trail, and their packsaddles and loads carried up the hill on the backs of soldiers and then reloaded, a time-consuming and exhausting process.

Airdrops were big events, especially if the men had been without rations for a day or two, but also dangerous, as the presence of the cargo planes gave away the Marauders' position. The battalion or combat team would assemble

BELOW LEFT
A decent hot breakfast was a rare treat. Captain Ossie Burch, a company commander, watches intently as Sergeant Morris Anderson cooks pancakes made from captured Japanese flour on an entrenching tool. Both men are wearing the light wool jerseys, and Anderson is wearing the special jungle boots provided to the Marauders. (Merrill's Marauders Association)

BELOW
River crossings were frequent. Walking in wet boots and wet clothes was uncomfortable and contributed to skin rashes. A Marauder drains water from his boots before moving on. (Merrill's Marauders Association)

near the drop zone, and wait while the cargo planes found the DZ and made their drops. As soon as the supplies were ready for distribution the men would march past collecting their rations and ammunition, while the mules and horses were quickly loaded and led back to the column. Every effort was made to clear the drop zone and get away as quickly as possible. If a supply drop had to be canceled, because of proximity to the Japanese, or weather, or communications failure, which was all too common in the mountains, then the Marauders did without rations until the next drop.

The day would end near sundown, unless there was farther to go, in which case the men marched on into the night. The columns tried to set up camp in and around the nearest high ground, but if no bivouac area had been selected, the men would simply move a few feet off the trail to bed down. Before dark patrols would go out to search the surrounding trails for any signs of the Japanese, while the platoons formed a perimeter around the bivouac area, digging foxholes and setting up machine guns to cover likely approaches of attack. After a quick supper there would be time for cleaning weapons and other equipment. The muleskinners would have to unload their mules and horses, arrange feed for them, and tend to any sores or wounds. The radio men

At the end of the day the columns would bivouac and set up a perimeter. A machine-gun position guards the trail while a patrol returns to the area. (Merrill's Marauders Association)

would be on the radios, often well into the night, checking with headquarters for orders, contacting the Intelligence and Reconnaissance Platoon for any intelligence, or setting up the next airdrop. There were few comforts. A soldier bedding down near the Communications Platoon might get to hear a news broadcast. Mail was intermittent, as the Marauders were not allowed to receive or send mail while they were behind enemy lines; they went without for more than two months. When they could, the supply section tried to include a few magazines or books in the supply drops, which were eagerly received and anticipated. On one occasion, the Marauders opened a package of rations to find, to their dismay, *The Pocket Book of Etiquette*, *Children's Book of Wild Animals*, and *The Boy Scout Handbook*.

Sleeping arrangements were simple, on whatever flat space that could be found. The men used a buddy system, sharing their ponchos and wool blankets.

In the bivouac area the men would bed down wherever they could. The ubiquitous bamboo provided material to make a quick shelter using a poncho or shelter half. (Merrill's Marauders Association)

One poncho would be put down on a cleared patch of ground, and a blanket placed over it, then two soldiers would cover themselves with the second blanket and the second poncho. At times, particularly if there was rain, the ponchos would be tied over a framework of bamboo to make a crude shelter. In the foxholes, one man slept while the other was on guard, then the positions reversed, through the night. Dawn would bring a new day, with more hills to climb, more jungle to march through, and growing fatigue.

Food

As the campaign wore on, food became an obsession. When the unit was being organized and its mission defined, the War Department decided that the Marauders would rely on K-rations as their principal source of food, to be supplemented, when possible, with C-rations, 10-in-1 meals, and B-rations. K-rations came in three waxed cardboard boxes, for breakfast, dinner, and supper, with the following contents:

Breakfast: two-ounce can of chopped ham and egg, K-1 biscuit, K-2 biscuit, fruit bar, coffee, sugar, four cigarettes, chewing gum, and chocolate-flavored D-ration bar.

Dinner: two-ounce can of processed cheese, K-1 and K-2 biscuits, malted milk tablets, powdered lemon juice, sugar tablets, four cigarettes, chewing gum, D-ration bar.

Supper: two-ounce can of processed meat, K-1 and K-2 biscuits, bouillon powder, four cigarettes, chewing gum, D-ration bar.

K-rations made up about 80 percent of the rations the Marauders received while on campaign. The advantage of K-rations was their versatility. They were lightweight, easily portable, and didn't require heating. A soldier could carry enough K-rations in his pack to last three days, and one parachute could drop 56 man-days of K-rations, which could feed a platoon for two days. K-rations, however, failed to provide an adequate calorific intake for the heavy physical exertion the men were undergoing nearly every day. A full day's K-ration pack contained 3,000 calories, which was totally inadequate. K-rations were designed as emergency food, not the basis of a sustained diet. As a result, the Marauders steadily lost weight. Charlton Ogburn recalled:

"We were perpetually famished. Not only were K-rations lacking in bulk, but every fourth or fifth day we ran out of them. We had two conditions: one in which we felt unfed, the other in which we were unfed."

Private 1st Class Edward Dempsey starts a small fire for breakfast while Private 1st Class Joseph Bannon eats from a can of C-rations, an infrequent but welcome break from the monotony of K-rations. (Merrill's Marauders Association)

With few other comforts or diversions, food was entertainment, something to look forward to and to talk about endlessly, recounting past meals and planning future ones. Sadly, there was little to break the monotony of eating K-rations. At times, a mistake in loading back at the Marauders' base would make the monotony worse when the airdropped rations would be opened and found to contain nothing but supper meals. With K-rations, it was less a question of which meal a soldier liked, and more which meal he loathed least. Breakfast was the prized meal, as it contained coffee, and the fruit bar could be slowly melted in a little water to make a sort of jam for the biscuits. Some thought the processed cheese from the dinner meal was palatable, while others couldn't stand it. At each mealtime there would be active trading of K-ration components, with cigarettes and sugar packets as key items of currency. The irregular drops of C-rations and 10-in-1 meals, usually when the Marauders had a day or two of rest, brought welcome relief and were a real boost to morale. If there were no Japanese in the area, it would be possible to go fishing in one of the many rivers. One soldier would walk upstream from his fellow fishermen who would remove their shirts to use as nets. A grenade thrown into the water would stun the fish, which would be collected in the shirts as they floated downstream, then cooked over an open fire. On several occasions the Marauders captured supplies of Japanese rice, flour, and other rations that were eagerly added to their own rations. When the Marauders exchanged their positions with Chinese troops, there would be an opportunity to trade American cigarettes for Chinese rice and tea. Adding a K-ration fruit bar and some sugar to rice made a passable pudding.

Health

Disease proved to be more of a danger to the Marauders than the Japanese. By the end of the campaign there were nearly five times as many casualties from disease as from combat. The area the Marauders fought over was rife with disease, while the heat, the humidity, the damp, and the strenuous marching on an inadequate diet sapped a soldier's strength and his health. The fatigue was never-ending. The combination of disease, exertion, fatigue, and poor diet led, inevitably, to complete exhaustion.

Malaria was endemic and despite regular use of Atabrine almost all of the Marauders contracted some form of malaria. Many of the Pacific veterans became re-infected. Dengue fever and typhus were present, as was the deadlier scrub typhus. Many succumbed to what were simply termed "Fevers of Unknown Origin," or F.U.O., which would leave a man burning with fever and aching in every joint as if he had been run over by a truck. The rivers and streams were contaminated with bacteria and parasites that caused diarrhea, bacillary, and amoebic dysentery. It was rarely possible for the Marauders to boil water to purify it; they relied instead on halazone tablets, but maintaining water purification discipline was often difficult. To be effective, the tablets had to be dissolved in a canteen for 30 minutes before drinking. In the heat of

Marauders refill their canteens from a jungle stream. These streams were a source of bacillary and amoebic dysentery. (Merrill's Marauders Association)

the day, having had a hard march all morning, not all soldiers could resist the temptation of a cool mountain stream. Some men would fill their canteens, drink them dry, and fill them up a second time, only then putting in the halazone tablets. Even for those who were disciplined, it was found that halazone could not destroy the amoeba that caused amoebic dysentery. Diarrhea was a common complaint, and amoebic dysentery became the second most frequent cause of medical evacuations. By the end of the campaign, the average weight loss was 20 pounds per man.

To add to the general discomfort, insects of all sorts flourished in the jungle. Mosquitoes, flies, gnats, and ticks were ever present, and often carried diseases. Several varieties of leech lay in wait, some dropping down from leaves above the trail, some attaching themselves as a man brushed past a bush. Leeches had to be found and removed promptly, or an open sore would result. In the heat and damp an insect bite, a leech bite, or a gash from a thorn or branch could quickly become infected, turning into what were called "Naga sores."

For the Marauders, life on campaign was a constant struggle, a struggle that continued regardless of whether or not they were in combat. The Marauders battled daily against the terrain and the environment, against disease, against their own hunger, and against their growing exhaustion. And then they faced the Japanese.

THE EXPERIENCE OF BATTLE

From February to the end of May 1944, the Marauders fought five major and 30 minor engagements with the Japanese. They spent countless hours patrolling and waiting in ambush along jungle trails. Most of their fighting was done at close range, often at less than 50 yards, half the distance of a football field. Their tactics served them well, enabling the Marauders to inflict severe casualties on the Japanese 18th Division. These tactics – "a swift approach march along an unguarded route; the retention of surprise; a hasty, accurate reconnaissance, followed by a bold attack against the enemy's weakness; and the employment of well-aimed, disciplined fires," as noted in Major Scott McMichael's *A Historical Perspective on Light Infantry* – were the keys to the Marauders' success. When the Marauders were forced into more conventional roles, where they were unable to utilize their superior mobility and the benefit of surprise, their lack of heavy weapons and supporting arms worked to their disadvantage. Their experience of combat under these circumstances, at the siege of Nhpum Ga and in the attempt to capture the town of Myitkyina, was grueling.

Patrolling and ambush
Logan Weston, who commanded the Intelligence & Reconnaissance Platoon in the 3rd Battalion, said that jungle fighting "was a matter of quick, close encounters where a fellow's life depended on his own cunning, speed, and skill." This is a good description of what the Marauders experienced while on patrol, triggering an ambush, or reacting to one. Patrolling was a constant activity. In the jungle both the Japanese and the Marauders were, in effect, blind, and as a blind person uses a stick and a gentle tapping to feel his or her way down a city street, both sides in this jungle war used patrols to feel out their enemy.

From the Hukwang Valley to Myitkyina, February 24–May 27, 1944

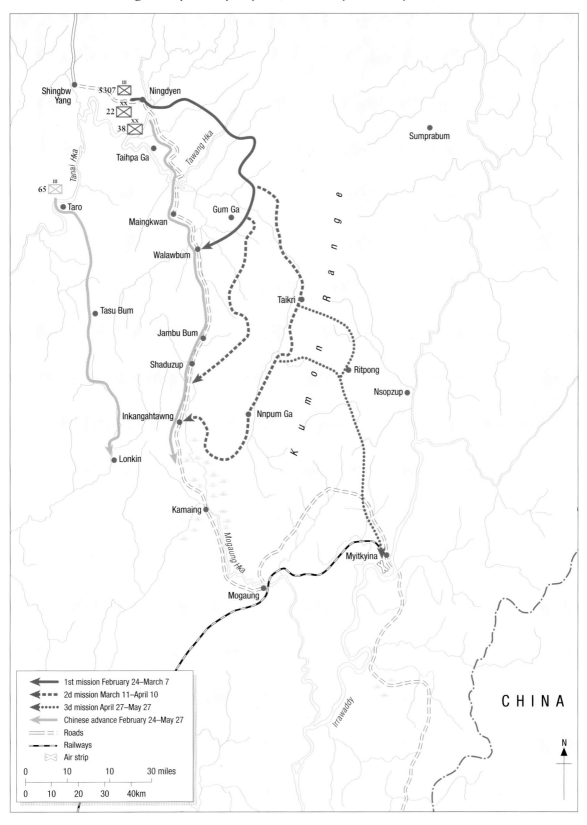

Shingbw Yang

5307 · Ningdyen

22

38

Taihpa Ga

Tanai Hka

Tawang Hka

65

Taro

Maingkwan

Gum Ga

Walawbum

Sumprabum

Tasu Bum

Taikri

Jambu Bum

Shaduzup

Ritpong

Nsopzup

Inkangahtawng

Nnpum Ga

K u m o n   R a n g e

Lonkin

Kamaing

Mogaung Hka

Myitkyina

Mogaung

Irrawaddy

CHINA

Legend:
- 1st mission February 24–March 7
- 2d mission March 11–April 10
- 3d mission April 27–May 27
- Chinese advance February 24–May 27
- Roads
- Railways
- Air strip

| 0 | 10 | 10 | 30 miles |
| 0 | 10 | 20 | 30 | 40km |

N

The Marauder columns sent out patrols to guard against surprise attacks and to locate the enemy. On a short patrol the men would take only ammunition and perhaps a canteen, to give optimum freedom of movement in the jungle. (Merrill's Marauders Association)

The Marauder battalions used their Intelligence and Reconnaissance Platoons to scout well ahead of the columns, but the columns sent out other patrols as well, moving just ahead of the column, and checking side trails. The men in the rifle companies, the heavy weapons platoons, and the pioneer and demolition platoons all undertook patrols in squad or platoon strength, alternating the duty. The standard formation for a platoon patrol was to have one or two men in the lead as scouts, followed by the platoon leader with the 1st Squad, then the 2nd Squad, then the 3rd Squad with the platoon sergeant, and two men following behind as a rearguard. Patrolling required what Charlton Ogburn called "nerve-straining vigilance," a constant alertness for any sign, any sound that might indicate the presence of the Japanese, to avoid becoming what the Pacific veterans cynically referred to as "Nambu bait." The entire patrol would scan the jungle constantly, to the left and to the right, checking the treetops for snipers, and the path for the telltale signs of the hobnailed or split-toed boots the Japanese soldiers wore. A boot print filling with water usually meant that the enemy had only recently passed by.

At regular intervals the patrol would stop and listen, waiting a few minutes before moving on down the trail. Moments of heightened tension came at every bend in the trail, or when the patrol came to an open area, or a deserted village, which would have to be carefully searched.

The men could never forget for a moment that they were both the hunters, and the hunted. When the Japanese became aware that the Marauders were in their area, they waited in ambush. The Japanese often set up an S-shaped formation of machine guns across a trail, with a few guns on each side of the trail to give a crossing fire. When an American patrol ran into the ambush, the Japanese soldiers would pin down the leading squad with machine-gun fire, then quickly bring their knee mortars into

Japanese S-shaped
machine-gun formation

TRAIL

action, firing down the trail to prevent the other squads from moving up in support. The Marauders developed, and practiced repeatedly, a standard procedure to deal with an ambush. On encountering an ambush, the lead squad would step off the trail and lay down a base of fire, while the two following squads would enter the jungle, one to the left of the trail and one to the right, pushing forward until they could converge on the flanks at the far end of the Japanese ambush, to either wipe out the Japanese troops or force them to abandon the position. Alertness and quick reactions, and the American advantage in automatic weapons, were the keys to survival.

Automatic weapons proved devastating when the Marauders ambushed the Japanese. Perhaps because the Marauders were operating so far behind the front lines, and were therefore unexpected, the Japanese soldiers were often quite casual while moving along the trails, sometimes to the point of carelessness. In some of the denser jungle an ambush party could be just a few feet off a trail and be completely invisible to an approaching enemy. As John George noted in *Shots Fired in Anger*, with their BARs, M1s, M1 carbines, and Thompsons, the Marauders could get off two to four shots before a Japanese soldier had hit the ground. Often small groups of Japanese were taken completely by surprise and were killed or wounded before they could return fire.

Ambushes were a regular feature of the Marauders' war. 1st Lieutenant Phil Piazza, Blue Combat Team, 2nd Battalion, searches a dead Japanese soldier caught in an ambush for documents. (Merrill's Marauders Association)

The Marauders' advantage in firepower usually proved decisive in an ambush. 1st Lieutenant Dominic Perrone, holding a Japanese bayonet, looks over three dead Japanese soldiers from a patrol his platoon had ambushed. (Merrill's Marauders Association)

The terrain often gave a significant advantage to the defender setting up an ambush, a factor the Japanese and the Marauders both used to their benefit at different times. The denser jungle and steeply sloping mountainsides restricted forward movement to a narrow band on either side of a trail or position. Rarely could more than one or two platoons be brought into action at the same time, which made flanking movements difficult. As a result, a small force could delay a much larger one. On the approach to Shaduzup, the 1st Battalion's leading platoons ran into a Japanese blocking force that retreated slowly, setting up successive blocks along the trail. After eight actions against this Japanese force, the platoons had managed to advance only a mile and a half, and the battalion was forced to cut a new route through the jungle, avoiding the trails altogether. A few weeks later, as the 2nd and 3rd Battalions were withdrawing toward Nhpum Ga, Lieutenant Logan Weston and his Intelligence and Reconnaissance Platoon, with one other rifle platoon under Lieutenant Warren Smith, held off a Japanese company for two full days along a series of razorback ridges.

E   **AMBUSH**

The ambush was a combat technique that both the Marauders and the Japanese employed in the jungle. In some of the terrain in northern Burma, the jungle growth was so thick that a man sitting two or three feet off a trail would be nearly invisible. Ambushes were hard to detect, which meant that survival required constant vigilance and lightning-quick reactions. The Marauders' automatic and semi-automatic weapons gave them a decided advantage over the Japanese in an ambush. Armed with an M1 Garand, a carbine, a Thompson, or a BAR, a Marauder could get off two to four shots before a Japanese soldier had a chance to react. The hours the Marauders spent in marksmanship training paid off in superior accuracy. The steep jungle-covered hills gave the ambusher an added advantage, making it more difficult for his opponents to move around his flanks, thus enabling a small force to hold off superior numbers.

Blocking force: the battles of Walawbum, Shaduzup, and Inkangahtawng

For their first and second missions, General Stilwell ordered the 5307th to sweep around the Japanese 18th Division's right flank and cut the Japanese supply line along the Kamaing road, creating an opportunity for Stilwell's Chinese 22nd and 38th Divisions to force the Japanese further back down the Hukwang Valley. Stilwell hoped that his "hammer and anvil" tactics would lead to the destruction of the Japanese 18th Division. By the third week of February the Chinese were moving toward the village of Maingkwan, roughly 20 miles from Ningbyen where the 5307th had assembled. Stilwell ordered Merrill to take the 5307th behind Japanese lines and cut the Kamaing road at the village of Walawbum, 12 miles south of Maingkwan. On February 24, 1944, the three battalions set out in columns of combat teams, with their Intelligence and Reconnaissance platoons working ahead probing for the Japanese 18th Division's right flank. Run-ins with several Japanese patrols, which resulted in the first Marauder killed in action, convinced Merrill that the Marauders had to swing farther to the east to get around the Japanese flank. A 40-mile march, during which the unit made three river crossings, brought the 5307th close to Walawbum by March 2, where Merrill ordered the 3rd Battalion to hold a stretch of higher ground on the east bank of a small river, the Numpyek, just east of the village and the Kamaing Road, covering the road with mortar and machine-gun fire. Merrill ordered the 2nd Battalion to cross the Numpyek River and set up a block on the Kamaing Road about two and a half miles to the west of Walawbum village; Merrill held the 1st Battalion in reserve, but had the battalion set up blocks along the trails leading to Walawbum.

The 3rd Battalion's two combat teams began moving toward their objective on March 3, with Orange Combat Team in the lead. The battalion's

A Marauder column passes through an abandoned group of huts on the way to Walawbum. (National Archives)

Intelligence and Reconnaissance platoon, under Lieutenant Logan Weston, crossed over to the west bank of the Numpyek River to cover Orange Combat Team's flank. Unsure of what they were facing, the next day the Japanese began probing the Marauders' positions. A force of 30 soldiers attacked Khaki Combat Team, while a larger force, estimated at 90 or more, hit Lieutenant Weston's platoon, which had dug in on a small section of higher ground. The platoon repelled five attacks, before withdrawing back across the river under cover of 81mm mortar fire and fire from Khaki Combat Team. These actions diverted attention from Orange Combat Team's advance to the river, where the Marauders set up a perimeter along a bluff on the east bank. Across the waist-deep water on the west bank a grass field gave way to trees and jungle beyond which lay Walawbum village and the Kamaing Road. Knowing what to expect, the Pacific veterans of Orange Combat Team broke out their entrenching tools and dug their foxholes deep, covering them with logs for added protection. From their foxholes the Marauders could hear the sounds of Japanese voices and trucks moving along the road. The combat team's heavy weapons platoon set up their 60mm and 81mm mortars and began firing on the village and the Kamaing Road. The Japanese soon replied with their own mortars, then sent over scattered artillery fire, but by then the Marauders were well protected.

The 2nd Battalion, meanwhile, had moved to the Kamaing Road west of Walawbum, having to cut a trail through the jungle and tall elephant grass. Reaching the road in the evening of March 4, the battalion quickly set up blocks covering the road with machine guns on both sides to give covering fire, with the Blue Combat Team to the north and Green Combat Team facing east back toward the village. The next morning, completely unaware that the Marauders were anywhere near the area, small groups of Japanese soldiers moving north and south along the road ran into the blocks and were quickly wiped out by machine-gun fire. Now alerted, the Japanese started firing on the 2nd Battalion's positions with mortars and artillery. During the day the Blue Combat Team fought off six infantry attacks, waiting until the Japanese had approached to close range before opening fire. That night, having held the block for 36 hours without food and running low on ammunition, and with intelligence that the Japanese were bringing up heavier artillery to bombard the block, the 2nd Battalion withdrew.

The men of Orange Combat Team spent the day in their foxholes under intermittent shelling. Two Japanese patrols attempted to attack the flanks of the position under mortar and artillery fire, but were thrown back, leaving more than 70 dead. All day long the combat team's 81mm mortars shelled concentrations of Japanese troops on the other side of the river, while the battalion's air liaison officer called in air strikes. Mustangs flew back and forth along the Kamaing Road, bombing and strafing. That night the Marauders could hear more Japanese trucks pulling up and the tailgates slamming down as reinforcements jumped off. The next day, March 6, the Japanese began shelling the Marauders' position shortly after dawn and around mid-morning added medium artillery fire. Sergeant Andrew Pung of the Heavy Weapons Platoon climbed up a tree overlooking the position and directed mortar fire on concentrations of Japanese troops, until he was stunned by a tree burst. The men knew an attack was coming. Toward the end of the afternoon the Japanese fire intensified, machine-gun and rifle fire from across the river joining the mortar and artillery rounds hitting Orange's position, keeping the Marauders pinned in their foxholes.

Chinese troops from the 38th Division move up to take over positions from the Marauders after their battle at Walawbum, March 7, 1944. (National Archives)

Then, remarkably, at 1715hrs the supporting fire stopped. A Japanese infantry company rose up and with shouts of "Banzai!" and other oaths charged toward the river, with another company following behind, an action that one Marauder recalled was "enough to scare the wits out of anybody involved in it." All the hours of intensive marksmanship training at Deogarh paid off. The Marauders waited until the front rank of the Japanese charge was about 40 yards away and about to enter the river before opening fire. The front rank of the Japanese collapsed under the weight of fire. With remarkable bravery, the charge continued. All through the attack, Sergeant Hank Gosho, a Nisei attached to Lieutenant Weston's Intelligence and Reconnaissance Platoon, continued to translate orders that Japanese officers were shouting to their men. The Marauders kept up a disciplined fire for nearly half an hour; the two heavy .30-cal. machine guns posted on each flank of the position fired off more than 5,000 rounds. Bizarrely, in the midst of this execution there were humorous moments. When, above the roar of firing, a Japanese voice could be heard yelling "Eleanor eats powdered eggs!" – a reference to President Franklin Roosevelt's wife – Major Peter Petito, second in command of Orange Combat Team, shouted back, in Japanese, "Tojo eats shit!" When all the firing had stopped 45 minutes later, some 400 Japanese soldiers lay dead. Three Marauders had been wounded in the attack. Shortly thereafter the Japanese withdrew back down the Kamaing Road. In the two actions around Walawbum the Marauders had lost eight men killed in action and 37 wounded, while killing an estimated 800 Japanese soldiers. On March 7, as the Marauders withdrew from the area, men of the Chinese 38th Division arrived to take up positions around Walawbum.

After a few days' rest and re-supply, the Marauders set off on their next mission. With the help of the 5307th, Stilwell's Chinese divisions had pushed the Japanese 18th Division out of the Hukwang Valley. The next stage was to gain control of the Mogaung Valley by forcing the Japanese off the Jambu Bum Ridge and pushing into the valley. Stilwell ordered the 5307th to make two envelopments. The 1st Battalion, followed by the 113th Regiment from the 38th Division, would make a shallow envelopment to block the Japanese supply route along the Kamaing Road at Shaduzup, south of the Jambu Bum Ridge. The 2nd and 3rd Battalions would make a wider, deeper envelopment, marching around 80 miles to cut the road farther south near the village of Inkangahtawng. The terrain was the most difficult the Marauders had yet encountered. To swing around the Japanese lines, the Marauders had to move into the western slopes of the Kumon mountain range, up and over a series of steep ridges that were a challenge to men and animals. The 2nd and 3rd Battalions would follow the valley of the Tenai River, which offered its own challenges and torments.

On March 12 the 1st Battalion set off on its trek to Shaduzup. Two days later the battalion's Intelligence and Reconnaissance Platoon, under Lieutenant Sam Wilson, ran into a stubborn Japanese force blocking the trail along the intended route. The Japanese were using their S-shaped ambush formation along the trail; when the Marauders pushed through the jungle to flank the

Japanese position, the Japanese would quickly withdraw, move a short way down the trail, and set up a new block. Lieutenant Colonel Osborne, 1st Battalion commander, realizing that the Japanese were now aware of the Marauders' presence, decided to use his Red Combat Team to contain the Japanese while his White Combat Team swung around the Japanese block by cutting a new trail through the jungle. Once the new trail had been cut, Red Combat Team would disengage and follow. The men of White Combat Team spent a back-breaking day cutting a trail in hot and humid weather through the thick jungle and bamboo up and over the mountain slopes. It took the battalion two days to move four miles. An airdrop scheduled for the 16th had to be postponed to the next day when the C-47s couldn't find the drop zone in the mountains, leaving the men without rations after their heavy exertion.

Pushing west, the battalion ran into further Japanese blocks along its intended route, losing several killed and wounded in firefights along the trails. Once again, Lieutenant Colonel Osborne decided to go off the main trails and cut a new route through the jungle. To get up the steep hillsides, the men had to unload the pack animals, carry the loads on their own backs up the hill, then go back down to bring the animals up. The battalion spent several days marching down the Chengun River, which offered a slightly easier approach, but the men remained wet constantly. When the battalion finally neared Shaduzup on March 26, Osborne learned that the Japanese had a company-sized force in a camp nearby, and another company to the south. He ordered Major Caifson Johnson's White Combat Team to make a night

Men of the 2nd and 3rd Battalions crossed this Kachin-built bridge over the Tanai River on March 18, 1944, on their way to Inkangahtawng. After crossing the bridge the Marauders faced a steep 2,000-foot climb. (National Archives)

attack on the camp across on the west bank of the Mogaung River, while Red Combat Team and the Chinese 113th Regiment held positions on the east bank. White Combat Team set off in three columns at 0300 on the morning of March 28. As the men waded silently across the river, they could hear Japanese soldiers talking and collecting water a few hundred yards downstream. As dawn broke, the Marauders of White Combat Team swept through the camp, firing and throwing grenades. The Japanese soldiers fled in confusion, leaving rice, potatoes, and fish cooking on their campfires. The Marauders eagerly devoured these Japanese rations.

White Combat Team quickly formed a perimeter around the camp, hurriedly digging foxholes, and set up blocks on the Kamaing Road to the north and south of the camp with light machine guns covering the approaches. To the south of the camp, an unsuspecting Japanese company moving up to the Jambu Bum ran into the Marauder road block, leaving 60 dead after being caught in a withering blast of fire. By mid-morning the Japanese had begun to react to the presence of the Marauders across their route to the south. Snipers started firing into the perimeter, then around mid-morning 75mm and 150mm artillery began to shell both the White Combat Team positions and Red Combat Team across the Mogaung River. The Marauders could hear the sound of trucks bringing up reinforcements. Around noon, the Japanese launched their first attack across an open field toward White Combat Team's perimeter, but were repulsed with heavy losses. Several more attacks took place during the afternoon, but made no headway against the Marauders' disciplined fire, backed up by the 81mm mortars of Red Combat Team. The Marauders estimated that several hundred Japanese soldiers had been killed in these attacks. The Japanese kept shelling the Marauders during the night, but the battle was effectively over. The next morning the 113th Regiment crossed the Mogaung River and took over the Marauders' positions, bringing up their own 75mm pack howitzers to shell the Japanese, who had begun retreating south toward Kamaing. General Merrill ordered the 1st Battalion to rejoin the 5307th further to the southeast.

The 2nd and 3rd Battalions had also started on their part of the mission on March 12, marching 20 miles east of Walawbum to the valley of the Tenai River, then working south down the narrow river valley, crossing the river several times in the process. After a week of following the Tenai River, the two battalions headed southwest into the mountains, making a difficult climb up to a ridge line that ran north and south at varying altitudes of between 1,500 and 3,000 feet. As the 1st Battalion had found, this was the most difficult terrain yet encountered, and the climbs and descents were exhausting. On March 21, General Merrill ordered Colonel Hunter to take the 2nd Battalion's two combat teams, Green and Blue, and Khaki Combat Team from the 3rd Battalion, and set up a block along the Kamaing Road near the village of Inkangahtawng, about 10 miles south of Shaduzup on the Mogaung River and 30 miles from their current position. The 3rd Battalion's Orange Combat Team would block the trails to the south of the 2nd Battalion's approach route to guard against a Japanese flanking movement.

Colonel Hunter's force descended from the mountain ridges to follow two small river gorges to their destination, crossing one river 25 times along the way. After reaching the Mogaung Valley, the force took an airdrop near the village of Manpin, then marched on through the night toward Inkangahtawng. Lieutenant Colonel McGee, commander of the 2nd Battalion, took his Green and Blue Combat Teams across the Mogaung River on the afternoon of March

23, setting up a perimeter a quarter of a mile north of Inkangahtawng and several hundred yards east of the Kamaing road. Khaki Combat Team remained on the east bank, setting up a perimeter with the 2nd Battalion's 60mm and 81mm mortars covering the defensive position on the west bank and the Kamaing Road. Ignoring their fatigue, Green and Blue Combat Teams quickly dug in while patrols went out to the north and south of the perimeter. It did not take long for the Japanese to realize that the Marauders had set up a roadblock. They soon began peppering the perimeter with intermittent rifle and mortar fire. All through the night the Marauders could hear the sound of Japanese trucks arriving with reinforcements, who were exceptionally noisy. The Marauders knew they would be hit at dawn, which is what happened.

At 0700 on March 24, the 2nd Battalion's west flank began taking heavy mortar fire, which lasted for 15 minutes. As the mortar fire slackened, the men heard the sounds of Japanese soldiers shouting as they charged through the high kunai grass and underbrush toward the Marauders' positions. With

1st Lieutenant Logan Weston, who commanded the 3rd Battalion's Intelligence and Reconnaissance Platoon. Weston's stubborn defense of the trails leading to Nhpum Ga, with the assistance of Lieutenant Smith and his platoon, enabled the 2nd and 3rd Battalions to make a successful withdrawal from Inkangahtawng. (Merrill's Marauders Association)

yells of "Banzai!" the Japanese charged forward. At a range of 20 yards the Marauder perimeter opened fire; none of the attackers in this initial charge survived. The Japanese quickly regrouped, and charged again and again in the face of murderous automatic fire. The 2nd Battalion's and Khaki Combat Teams mortars fired on the Japanese assembly areas from across the Mogaung River. For the Marauders on the perimeter, it was a matter of keeping their heads down while putting out a heavy weight of fire against each attack. The Japanese soon switched their attacks to the north side of the perimeter, bringing up artillery to fire on the Marauders from close range, so close that the report of the gun and the explosion of its shell were almost simultaneous. The attacks from the north continued for three hours, without success. The Japanese then began attacking from the south, increasing their mortar and artillery fire into the perimeter. Lacking any artillery of its own, the battalion managed to get a request for air support out in the afternoon, which brought four P-51 Mustangs in to bomb and strafe the Japanese artillery positions.

By the end of the day the Marauders had repulsed 16 Japanese attacks, but they were running low on ammunition and could hear trucks bringing up more reinforcements. Lieutenant Colonel McGee learned that the 1st Battalion had not yet moved into its blocking position around Shaduzup, which meant that the Japanese could press the 2nd Battalion's position from the north and the south, potentially cutting off the battalion completely. McGee requested an urgent airdrop of ammunition, but was instead ordered to withdraw back across the Mogaung and disengage; his orders had been to hold his block for 24 hours, but not at the risk of being overwhelmed. The 2nd Battalion had suffered two men killed in action and 12 wounded, while the Japanese had lost over 200 killed, once again demonstrating the crippling effect of the Marauders' superior firepower on the Japanese offensive tactic of unsupported infantry charges. That evening the battalion withdrew across the river under covering fire from the 81mm mortars.

The siege of Nhpum Ga

As the 2nd Battalion and Khaki Combat Team were withdrawing from their block at Inkangahtawng, General Merrill received intelligence that a strong Japanese force was moving north from Kamaing up the valley of the Tenai River to attack the flanks of the Chinese 22nd Division near Shaduzup. This force was composed of two companies from the Japanese 114th Regiment and 600 men from the Japanese 55th Regiment, who were later joined by a second battalion from the Japanese 114th Regiment. Stillwell told Merrill to stop this force moving beyond Nhpum Ga, which would entail setting up and holding a fixed defensive position. As the US Army's official history noted, "this use of the 5307th in a static defensive role was a radical change in the concept of its employment" and not what the Marauders had been trained or equipped for. Merrill ordered Colonel Hunter to pull the 2nd Battalion and Khaki Combat Team back to Nhpum Ga with all speed, while Orange Combat Team blocked the trails leading from Kamaing to Nhpum Ga. The 1st Battalion was still engaged on its mission to set up the block at Shaduzup and could not be called on.

As the Marauders started back up the trails into the mountains carrying their wounded, it began to rain, in torrents. The trails quickly became muddy, making for hard going. Holes had to be cut in the canvas litters to let the rainwater drain off the wounded. Climbing back up the river gorge the Marauders had descended a few days before proved to be far more difficult for both men and pack animals, and exhausting, but there was no time to rest. The men had to cross and re-cross the river over 40 times in the heat. Between the rain and the river, the Marauders were constantly wet. Airdrops provided badly needed supplies of K-rations and ammunition, while light planes braved the deteriorating weather to evacuate the wounded. Hunter's force arrived at the village of Manpin on March 26, where Khaki Combat Team rejoined the 3rd Battalion. The two battalions set off for Nhpum Ga, continuing their forced march, while two of the 3rd Battalion's platoons fought a remarkable delaying action.

To protect Hunter's lines of communication back from Inkangahtawng, before the attack Lieutenant Colonel Beach, 3rd Battalion commander, had sent Lieutenant Weston and his Intelligence and Reconnaissance Platoon south to block the trails leading to Manpin and on to Nhpum Ga from Kamaing. Weston, with 42 men, a section of light machine guns, and a section of 60mm mortars, moved four miles south on March 24 to the village of Poakum where the platoon dug in on high ground. Weston sent half a squad about three-quarters of a mile south of the village to set up an ambush along the trail to Kamaing. The 2nd Battalion's attack at Inkangahtawng prompted the Japanese to send a strong patrol north to cut off the battalion's retreat. In the early afternoon a patrol of 12 Japanese soldiers with a scout dog ran into Weston's half squad's ambush. All 12 were killed. Weston's men withdrew back to the platoon. Shortly thereafter a Japanese infantry company attacked Weston's position, but was forced back with heavy losses. All through the night Weston's men fought Japanese soldiers trying to infiltrate their positions by hurling grenades at the sound of movement, avoiding firing so as not to give away their positions. At dawn the next day the Japanese attacked Weston's position in force, but pulled back a few hours later. That afternoon Weston met up with Lieutenant Warren Smith and his rifle platoon, whom Lieutenant Colonel Beach had sent to assist Weston. Weston had Smith and his platoon dig in at a good position along a trail to the east to protect their withdrawal route.

After another uncomfortable night listening to Japanese patrols, in the early morning of March 26 Weston pulled his platoon back to another prepared position, leaving several of his wounded mules and fires burning in his old position. He and his platoon were soon rewarded with the sounds of two Japanese forces making frontal attacks on the positions they had just vacated, firing into each other. The Japanese soon recovered and attacked Weston's new position later in the morning, which the position halted with mortar fire. Around the same time a force of 100 Japanese ran into Lieutenant Smith's ambush and was forced back without loss to the Marauders. That afternoon Weston's platoon fought off a heavy assault that came from three sides. Realizing that he was in danger of being cut off, Weston withdrew his platoon under the cover of heavy mortar fire, pulling back to the village of Warong where he met up with Smith's platoon. Between them, they had 90 men available.

The next day, the Japanese probed Weston's and Smith's positions. These probing attacks were easily beaten off, but the Japanese began shelling the positions and were clearly building up for a heavier assault. Once again in danger of being cut off, Weston and Smith withdrew in a series of leapfrogs, one platoon holding the trail while the other moved back to set up a new defensive position. In this way they made good their escape, holding off the Japanese advance and rejoining the 3rd Battalion on its way north. In three days of fighting Weston and Smith had held off a much larger force of Japanese, taking every advantage of the terrain, and giving the 2nd and 3rd Battalions time to withdraw. The two platoons had killed more than 90 Japanese soldiers and wounded an estimated 150 more, at no loss to themselves.

General Merrill sent the 3rd Battalion four miles north of Nhpum Ga near the village at Hsamshingyang to hold a broad clearing that could be used for airdrops and evacuations and to block the trails leading north. The 2nd Battalion headed for Nhpum Ga, racing the fast-approaching Japanese up the trail along a razor-backed ridge to the few huts that constituted the village. On the morning of March 28, as the battalion started its march, Japanese artillery began shelling the trail, killing one Marauder and wounding several more. The

Sergeant George Feltwell, left, and Technical Sergeant J.C. Price, spent their birthdays together in the same foxhole during the siege of Nhpum Ga. The Marauders' Thompsons and BARs inflicted heavy casualties on the Japanese as they charged the Marauders' positions from short ranges. (Merrill's Marauders Association)

Withdrawal from Inkangahtawng, 2nd and 3rd Battalions, March 24–28, 1944

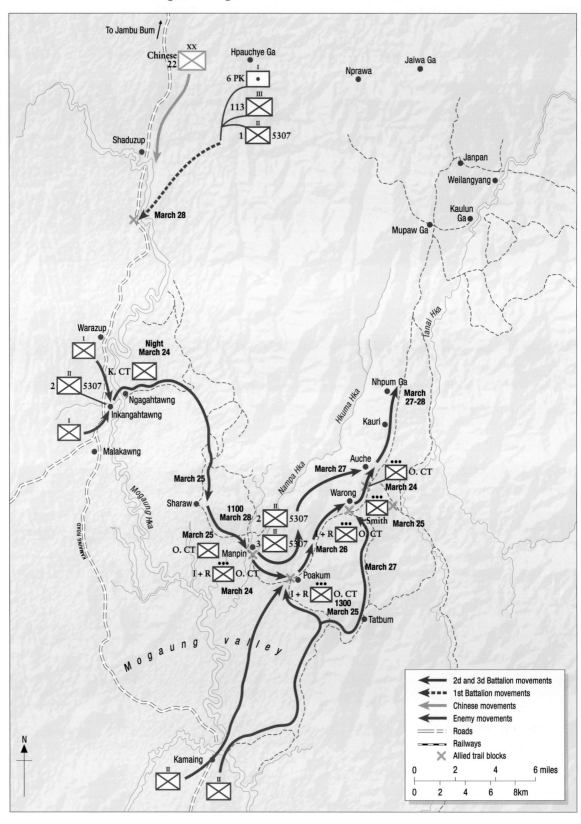

men raced up the muddy trail under constant fire, dropping in the mud as they heard an artillery round coming in. They reached Nhpum Ga just in time. Lieutenant Colonel McGee hurriedly set up a figure-eight defensive position around the two knolls at the top of the ridge line, an area of roughly 200 yards wide by 300 yards deep, with steep valleys falling away on either side. Green Combat Team took up positions in the northern half of the position, while Blue Combat Team took the southern half. While the men of Green and Blue Combat Teams dug in, a platoon and machine-gun detachment went back down the trail to delay the advancing Japanese, successfully ambushing several Japanese patrols as they withdrew back to the perimeter. That afternoon Japanese artillery began shelling the Marauders' position and sent in a probing attack, which was easily repulsed.

The next day, March 29, the fighting at Nhpum Ga began in earnest. After an artillery and mortar barrage, the Japanese attacked Blue Combat Team's positions from the southeast at 0600, from the southwest at 1000, and from due south at 1500, and at 1750 from the southwest again. All these attacks were pushed back with heavy losses. That same day, General Merrill was evacuated having experienced a heart attack, leaving Colonel Hunter in overall command. On March 30, the Japanese shifted their attacks to the east side of the perimeter, attacking several times during the course of the day. All the fighting was at close range. The Japanese soldiers would come pouring out of the jungle toward the Marauders' positions, some 20 or 30 yards away. From their well-dug foxholes, the Marauders would pour out a withering fire, breaking up each attack before it could reach the perimeter, but the attacks continued. On the 31st, in a series of heavy simultaneous attacks from the south, east, and northwest, the Japanese pushed back Green Combat Team and captured the one waterhole available and cut the trail back to the 3rd Battalion at Hsamshingyang. The 2nd Battalion was now surrounded.

Conditions within the perimeter steadily worsened. Japanese artillery and mortar fire had played havoc with the 2nd Battalion's pack animals, killing over 70, but at the same time preventing their disposal. In the heat the bodies of the animals began to rot, as did the bodies of the countless Japanese soldiers killed along the perimeter. The lack of water was the worst part of the ordeal. With the loss of the waterhole, the only water available was what could be collected from pools of rainwater, liberally flavored with dead mule. K-ration coffee did little to alter the taste. Lieutenant Colonel McGee had to call for an emergency airdrop of plastic water containers. The C-47 transports came in low to drop supplies of ammunition and rations right on top of the 2nd Battalion's positions. On one drop the men found to their delight that the base supply unit had sent them a meal of fried chicken, apple turnovers, and fresh bread and jam. Movement around the perimeter was difficult by day or night. Japanese snipers fired at any sight or sound. To remove a particularly annoying sniper firing on his aid station, Captain Abraham Kolodny, one of the 2nd Battalion's surgeons, bet a bazooka man $5 that he could not hit the sniper in the tree overlooking the aid station's position. The bazooka man took up his weapon, fired, and collected the $5 from the doctor.

When the weather permitted, P-51 Mustangs bombed and strafed Japanese positions under the control of the 2nd Battalion's air liaison officer within the perimeter. The 3rd Battalion had begun to push its way back down the trail from Hsamshingyang, but ran into heavily defended blocks along the steep trail back up to Nhpum Ga, which slowed down their advance. To give the 2nd Battalion more direct support, after his evacuation to hospital

A Marauder bids farewell to a friend at a temporary cemetery set up after the siege of Nhpum Ga. The Marauders lost 57 men killed and 302 wounded during the battle. (Merrill's Marauders Association)

General Merrill had arranged for two 75mm pack howitzers to be airdropped to the 3rd Battalion. Sergeant John Acker, who had fought with the 98th Field Artillery in New Guinea, was asked to form two gun teams from men with artillery experience. The guns arrived on April 2, and within two hours Sergeant Acker and his team had them assembled and firing into the Japanese positions around Nhpum Ga, giving the 2nd Battalion a real boost to morale. Colonel Hunter ordered the 1st Battalion, having completed its block at Shaduzup, to make a forced march to Hsimshangyang to add its weight to the attack.

It took another week to break the siege. The 2nd Battalion fought off repeated attacks by day and by night. By the ninth day, the battalion had suffered 17 men killed and 97 wounded, who could not be evacuated. The 3rd Battalion kept pushing hard toward Nhpum Ga, sending its two combat teams on flanking maneuvers to relieve the pressure of Japanese attacks on the 2nd Battalion. The terrain favored the Japanese defenders, as the hillsides were so steep that rarely could more than a platoon be brought to bear against a Japanese position, with the men having to claw their way through thick jungle up the slopes to flank the Japanese, working against machine-gun fire and grenades coming down on them. The gains were measured in yards. On April 7, an exhausted 1st Battalion arrived. Colonel Hunter had the battalion put together a team of 250 of the fittest men to aid a major attack the next day. Hunter sent Khaki Combat Team down the trail toward Nhpum Ga, while Orange Combat Team made a flanking movement to attack the Japanese on the east side of the 2nd Battalion's perimeter. The 1st Battalion's team marched through the jungle to create a diversionary attack on the Japanese positions south of Nhpum Ga. Khaki Combat Team had a rough day, continuing to meet heavy resistance along the trail, but the combined pressure of three attacks proved successful in forcing the Japanese to withdraw. The next morning, April 9, patrols from Khaki Combat Team moved down the trail without opposition and walked into the 2nd Battalion's perimeter. The 2nd Battalion withdrew to Hsamshingyang to rest and evacuate its wounded while the 1st and 3rd Battalions continued to patrol the area. The 2nd Battalion had held off a much larger Japanese force, estimated at more than two battalions, preventing the Japanese from their intention of attacking the flanks of the Chinese forces. The three Marauder battalions had managed to inflict heavy casualties on the Japanese, who lost more than 400 dead in their attacks, but the Marauders had suffered 57 men killed and 379 who had to be evacuated with wounds or disease, casualties the 5307th could ill afford.

To Myitkyina and the end

For two weeks following the lifting of the siege at Nhpum Ga, the 5307th remained in the general area, actively patrolling and setting up trail blocks to ensure that the Japanese did not return. The men received new uniforms and equipment, the first mail they had seen for months, and rested as best they

After lifting the siege at Nhpum Ga, the Marauders had a brief respite before their next mission, the capture of the airfield at Myitkyina. Major Edwin Briggs, commanding officer of Khaki Combat Team, 3rd Battalion, conducts a full inspection of his men. (National Archives)

could. The Marauders were exhausted. They had been through a month of back-breaking marches and hard fighting; dysentery was now common, many suffered from fevers and jungle sores, and every man had lost considerable weight on the K-ration diet. Evacuations for wounds and disease had steadily diminished the ranks. The 2nd Battalion had suffered the most. The battalion had been reduced to 472 men and had to be completely reorganized. The 1st and 3rd Battalions had not had the same level of casualties, but were still well below their original strength. The 5307th had roughly 1,600 men available, with no chance of getting replacements.

General Stilwell needed the Marauders for a third mission. The Japanese forces in northern Burma were coming under increasing pressure. Stilwell's Chinese divisions were moving down the Hukwang Valley and were 20 miles from Kamaing, the gateway to the Burma Railway and the Irrawaddy Valley. The British 3rd Division, Wingate's Chindits, were cutting the Japanese lines of communication to Myitkyina and tying up Japanese troops that might otherwise have been sent north to slow the Chinese advance. The main Japanese 15th Army was heavily involved battling the British 14th Army at Imphal and could spare no reinforcements for the hard-pressed Japanese 18th Division. The prize remained Myitkyina with its all-weather airstrip, but Stilwell needed to take it before the monsoon rains. He decided to use the 5307th, reinforced with two Chinese regiments and Kachin irregulars in an operation he dubbed END RUN. Merrill and Hunter developed a plan whereby two combat teams, H Force under Hunter, consisting of the 1st Battalion and the 150th Regiment of the Chinese 50th Division, and K Force under Colonel Henry Kinnison, from Stilwell's staff, consisting of the 3rd Battalion and the 88th Regiment, Chinese 30th Division, would cross over the 6,500-foot Naura Hkyet Pass in the Kumon Mountains and then converge on Myitkyina. M Force, under Lieutenant

A Marauder column near Myitkyina. Wracked with fever and dysentery, many of the men were by now on the verge of complete physical exhaustion after three months in the jungle. (Merrill's Marauders Association)

Colonel McGee, consisting of the reduced 2nd Battalion and 300 Kachin fighters, would move to the south of the main forces to cover their advance. Stilwell's orders to Merrill were to take and hold the airstrip at Myitkyina. Merrill told his officers that after the capture of the airstrip the Marauders would be flown out. This apparent promise soon became common knowledge among the men, and became the incentive for many to keep going well beyond the point of physical exhaustion.

The march to Myitkyina was, as one Marauder remembered, "a trail of sadness all the way through." K Force left the jumping-off point on April 28, with H Force following two days later. The route over the Naura Hkyat Pass followed a Kachin path that had not been used for a decade or more. The path climbed to the summit of the pass at 6,500 feet through a series of steep ascents. The rain turned the track to mud. Steps had to be cut into the sides of the mountain trail to help the mules climb, while the men carried their loads up to the next stage. Even then some mules slipped and fell to their death down the steep mountainsides, carrying with them badly needed weapons and ammunition. At night the men ate and slept on the trail, leaning their backs against the mountainside. Once over the pass, the path descended to the eastern slopes of the Kumon range which, though at lower altitude, were still exhausting to climb in the oppressive heat. Standard procedure had been to take a 10-minute break every hour while on the march; there were sections on the way to Myitkyina where the men had to take a break every 15 minutes, but they kept on. Wracked with dysentery, some men had resorted to cutting out the seats of their pants, which made their agony easier to deal with.

After defeating a Japanese force at the village of Ritpong on May 6–8, K Force attacked the Japanese-held village of Tingkrukawng to the southeast as a diversion for H Force's advance to Myitkyina. Hunter and his men reached a position four miles from the airstrip on May 16. After sending in a small patrol to reconnoiter the strip, Hunter began his attack at 1000 on May 17. The attack came as a complete surprise; by noon, H Force had captured the airstrip and several key points nearby. It appeared to Hunter that Myitkyina was only lightly defended, so he decided to make an effort to seize the town before the Japanese could bring in reinforcements. He called for K Force and M Force to get to Myitkyina as fast as possible, and urgently requested more troops and supplies from Merrill.

THE ATTACK ON MCLOGAN'S HILL

At the siege of Nhpum Ga, where the 2nd Battalion held off a much larger force of Japanese for some 12 days, the battalion's Nisei interpreters demonstrated remarkable bravery in defense of their comrades, regularly going outside the Marauder perimeter at night to listen to the Japanese. On the night of April 5/6, Sergeant Roy Matsumoto, armed only with a bayonet, crawled close to the Japanese positions. Matsumoto overheard the Japanese discussing an attack planned for the next morning at dawn on the position held by Lieutenant McLogan and his platoon. With this intelligence McLogan planned a trap. He had 20 men holding a small section of hillside below the crest of a ridge that sloped downhill to the jungle where the Japanese were gathering for their attack. McLogan pulled his men back to the ridge line, booby-trapped the vacated foxholes, and brought forward all his Thompson gunners and BAR men. When the Japanese attacked they quickly reached the empty foxholes where they hesitated for a moment. Sergeant Matsumoto immediately stood up in his foxhole on the ridge and shouted orders to the Japanese troops to charge forward. In the firing and confusion the Japanese followed his commands, charging up the hill and running into a storm of fire and grenades from the Marauders on the ridge. When the attack ended the Marauders counted 54 Japanese dead below them.

The vital airfield at Myitkyina, later in the battle. A C-47 takes off over P-40Ns of the 88th Fighter Squadron. During the siege of Myitkyina the fighter pilots would fly as many as six missions a day. (National Archives)

Unfortunately, through a series of errors and poor organization, the opportunity for the swift capture of Myitkyina evaporated. General Stilwell, who was exultant at the capture of the airstrip, had failed to put in place a plan for the capture of the town itself. In an attempt to take the town on May 17 and again the next day, two battalions of the 150th Regiment became confused and ended up firing on each other causing heavy casualties. Instead of the troops, ammunition, and rations that Hunter badly needed, the Army Air Force flew in an aviation engineer battalion to improve the strip and a battalion of British anti-aircraft troops to defend it. The delays enabled the Japanese commander at Myitkyina to bring in more reinforcements faster than Stilwell did, throwing the Marauders and the Chinese on the defensive. Expecting to be flown out once the airstrip had been taken, the Marauders now found themselves in a desperate fight to hold on to it.

Most of the Marauders were now completely worn out, but Stilwell apparently felt he could not order the relief of the 5307th while he was keeping

A Marauder water-cooled .30-cal. machine gun fires on Japanese troops near Singapur in defense of the Mytikyina airstrip. (National Archives)

A group of exhausted Marauders is evacuated to rear area hospitals. Many of the men were suffering from multiple illnesses. (National Archives)

the equally exhausted Chindits and his Chinese forces in combat, so they continued fighting. Stilwell set up a new command, the Myitkyina Task Force, to control the American and Chinese troops fighting for the town. General Merrill was again ill, so Colonel Hunter once again assumed command and the Marauder battalions were returned to his control. While the 1st Battalion helped defend the vital airstrip, the 2nd and 3rd Battalions took over sectors to the northwest. The physical condition of all three battalions was rapidly deteriorating. Medical evacuations rose alarmingly, despite pressure on the medical officers to keep evacuations to a minimum. In a controversial and bitterly resented move, convalescent hospitals were combed for replacements and 200 Marauders were sent back to Myitkyina, most of whom were unfit for combat duty.

During the last week of May the Marauders fought their final actions of the campaign, fighting off determined Japanese attacks, but they had exhausted what reserves of physical strength and morale they had left. Men

About 200 men from the 1st Battalion continued fighting at Myitkyina, with new replacements, until the town was captured on August 3, 1944. A platoon leader briefs his men before an attack toward the end of July. (National Archives)

were falling asleep in the middle of firefights. After months of eating only K-rations, many men could only tolerate the K-ration breakfast meal, vomiting up any other kind of food. By the end of May, the 2nd Battalion had been reduced to just 12 men fit for action. Lieutenant Colonel McGee requested that his battalion be relieved as it was no longer effective. The 3rd Battalion could muster 50 men fit for combat. Around 200 officers and men remained in the 1st Battalion. Stilwell finally had to accept the fact that, as he wrote in his diary, "GALAHAD is just shot."

AFTERMATH

Myitkyina did not fall until August 3, 1944 two months after most of the Marauders had been withdrawn from combat. At the end, there were still some 200 original Marauders in the lines. The rest had been evacuated to hospitals in and around Ledo for what would be weeks and in some cases months in recovery. The men were examined at the Myitkyina airstrip, given a tag that identified their main wounds or diseases, and flown out on waiting C-47s. At the hospitals, the men could bathe, wear clean clothes and eat decent food, and sleep in a bed for the first time in months. Most of the men who were evacuated suffered from multiple afflictions. Once released from hospital, the men were sent to a convalescent area, where at first the accommodation and conditions were not much better than what they had experienced living in the jungle, much to the disgust of the Marauders. Their treatment reinforced their feelings of bitterness toward the theater command.

Once back in India the men learned that the 5307th had become famous, and was now commonly known as "Merrill's Marauders." Shortly after the fall of Myitkyina came word that the 5307th had been awarded the Distinguished Unit Citation for its contribution to the campaign in northern Burma and the seizure of the airstrip at Myitkyina. During the course of their three missions the Marauders had suffered 424 battle casualties, with 93 men killed in action and 293 wounded who required hospitalization (many others with light wounds simply returned to duty), but 1,970 casualties from disease, a total casualty rate of 80 percent, close to what the War Department had predicted. But the Marauders had inflicted, proportionally, far greater losses on the Japanese.

G **AFTER THE BATTLE**

Myitkyina proved to be the Marauders' calvary. Of the 1,310 Marauders who reached the Myitkyina area on May 17, more than half had been evacuated by June 1, pushed beyond their physical and mental limits. Most of the rest followed shortly thereafter. When they could go no farther, the men were evacuated on C-47 transports to rear area hospitals in Assam. A flight of a few hours took them over the hills and jungle they had covered on foot over the previous three and a half months. Most were suffering from multiple afflictions, in addition to complete exhaustion. Recuperation took weeks. To the disgust and fury of the Marauders' medical officers, conditions in the convalescent camps left much to be desired. And to the disgust of the men, neither Merrill nor Stilwell bothered to visit them to offer their thanks or a word of appreciation. With the Marauders collapsing from exhaustion, General Stilwell rushed two battalions of combat engineers to Myitkyina to replace them, and then flew in a group of American infantry replacements that had recently arrived in India. These replacements went to form two battalions, designated "New Galahad." Additional regiments from the Chinese 30th and 50th Divisions joined the fighting. The capture of Myitkyina ultimately cost the American and Chinese forces 1,244 men killed and 4,139 men wounded, mostly among the Chinese troops.

And as the War Department had planned from the beginning, the 5307th Composite Unit (Provisional) was not reconstituted. The unit's end came as quickly as its formation, but not without controversy. The physical collapse of the Marauders at the end of their campaign, and the pressure to send sick men back to Myitkyina from hospitals only came to light after the fall of the town. Reports of these events in the American press were an embarrassment to General Stilwell, who was forced to order a full investigation.

On August 10, 1944, the 5307th was dissolved. There was no ceremony, no final parade or granting of individual awards. Shortly after the fall of Myitkyina Colonel Hunter, who had done so much to make the Marauders a successful combat unit, was dismissed as commander of American forces at Myitkyina and sent back to the United States by boat. A War Department ruling that all men who had served overseas for two or more years were eligible for immediate return to the United States applied to almost all the men in the 2nd and 3rd Battalions, who began to depart from India in August, taking with them an unofficial unit patch that they wore with pride. The men remaining in the 1st Battalion, together with replacements flown into Myitkyina after most of the Marauders had left, were organized into the 475th Infantry Regiment, under the command of Colonel William Osborne, the 1st Battalion's commander. As part of the Mars Force, the 475th continued the fight past Myitkyina, pushing the Japanese past Lashio and re-opening the Burma Road.

While he was convalescing in India, Charlton Ogburn composed a poem to the Marauders expressing the sentiments that many shared. Among the verses were the following:

Comes a line of weary scarecrows,
Bearded, pale, unclean, and hot.
Never would you think them soldiers
(Which we wish that we were not).
"Damn the mountains!" How we curse them!
"Damn the food, or what there is.
"Damn the mules, and General (Censored),
"God, we wish our feet were his!"...

Let the fevers try to stop us;
We've got dysentery now;
Still we'll keep the column rolling,
Though we could not say just how.
Half a thousand miles we've walked,
Over hills in rain and heat,
And the marches all have measured
That much more of Jap retreat.

For Merrill's men are marching;
We have come both fast and far,
And we've opened northern Burma
From Maingkwan to Myitkyina;
And there'll be no final halting
(So we fear it's bound to be)
Till the last mule's legs have buckled
Or we've reached the China Sea.

After weeks of rest and recuperation following the end of their campaign, most of the men in the 2nd and 3rd Battalions rotated back to the United States. Sergeant Michael Reising, left, and Sergeant Donald Ross, center, show some of the souvenirs they acquired in Burma. (National Archives)

BIBLIOGRAPHY

Bidwell, Shelford, *The Chindit War: The Campaign in Burma, 1944*, (Hodder & Stoughton, London 1979)

Bjorge, Gary J., *Merrill's Marauders: Combined Operations in Northern Burma in 1944* (Combat Studies Institute, US Army Command and General Staff College, Ft. Leavenworth, 1996)

George, Lieutenant Colonel John B., *Shots Fired in Anger*, second edition, revised and expanded (National Rifle Association, Washington, DC, 1981)

Hopkins, James E.T., in collaboration with John M. Jones, *Spearhead: A Complete History of Merrill's Marauders Rangers* (Galahad Press, Baltimore 1999)

Hunter, Colonel Charles Newton, *Galahad* (The Naylor Company, San Antonio, 1963)

Kirby, Major General S. Woodburn, *The War Against Japan, Volume III: The Decisive Battles* (HSMO, London 1961)

McMichael, Major Scott R., *A Historical Perspective on Light Industry*, Research Survey No. 6, (Combat Studies Institute, US Army Command and General Staff College, Ft. Leavenworth, 1987)

Ogburn, Charlton, Jr., *The Marauders* (Harper & Brothers, New York 1959)

Randolph, John, *Marsmen in Burma* (Gulf Publishing Company, Houston, 1946)

Romanus, Charles F. and Riley Sunderland, *United States Army in World War II: The China-Burma-India Theater: Stilwell's Command Problems*, (USGPO, Washington, DC 1956)

Stone, James H. (ed.), *Crisis Fleeting: Original Reports on Military Medicine in India and Burma in the Second World War* (USGPO, Washington, DC, 1969)

Sykes, Christopher, *Orde Wingate: A Biography* (The World Publishing Company, Cleveland, Ohio, 1959)

Weston, Colonel Logan E., *The Fighting Preacher* (Mountain Church, 2001)

United States War Department, General Staff: *Merrill's Marauders (February–May 1944)*, (USGPO, 1945)

INDEX